DYNAMICS OF BIBLICAL COUNSELING

SECOND EDITION

Nicolas André Ellen, PhD

ECTC

Expository Counseling Training Center

Houston, Texas

Publisher's Cataloging in Publication

Ellen, Nicolas: *Dynamics of Biblical Counseling Second Edition*
1. Counseling 2. Christian Counseling 3. Christianity 4. Discipleship
ISBN: 978-1-952902-06-2 (pbk.)
ISBN: 978-1-952902-07-9 (eBook)

Published by Expository Counseling Training Center
Houston, Texas
https://MyCounselingCorner.com

Contents

Section 1

Every Christian a Counselor 5

Section 2

Lessons I Have Learned in Counseling 15

Section 3

The Big Picture for Biblical Counseling 21

Section 4

Policies / Consent to Counsel / Personal Data Inventory 27

Section 5

The Eight Cs of Biblical Counseling / The Initial Counseling Session 45

Section 6

The Cul-de-Sacs of Life / Tracks of Counseling 53

Section 7

Sample of Data Gathering / Case Report Form 65

Section 8

When Encouragement Is Not Enough 69

Section 9

Biblical Hope 73

CONTENTS

Section 10

A Biblical Perspective on Emotions   **77**

Section 11

Understanding and Working through Suffering and Sorrow   **85**

Section 12

What You Cannot and Can Control   **93**

Section 13

The Point of Choice   **97**

Section 14

Developing in Love for God and Love for Others   **109**

Various Resources   **119**

Bibliography   **121**

Every Christian a Counselor

I. God is saving **souls** from the power, penalty, and soon the presence of sin (Eph. 2:1-10, Col. 1:12-14).

II. God is maturing **saints** into the image of Jesus Christ (2 Cor. 3:18, Rom. 8:29-30).

III. God is using the **Church** through evangelism to save souls (2 Cor. 5:18-20, Col. 1:3-6).

IV. God is using the **Church** through discipleship to mature saints into the image of Christ (Matt. 28:18-20, Eph. 4:11-15).

V. Biblical counseling is an **avenue** whereby evangelism and discipleship can take place, resulting in God's using it to save a soul from the power, penalty, and soon the presence of sin and maturing saints into the image of Jesus Christ. Therefore, every Christian should be a counselor!

VI. All good biblical counseling is built around guiding people into knowing God intimately, becoming like Him in character, and being useful to Him in service to others by

  A. Helping people establish a right relationship with God the Father through putting their faith in the person and work of Jesus Christ.

B. Helping people understand and address the motivations of their hearts.

C. Helping people put off particular sins that keep them from loving God and loving others.

D. Helping people put on particular patterns of righteousness that produce a love for God and love for others.

E. Providing wisdom to guide people into discerning and choosing the best course of action in a situation.

F. Consoling those who are suffering with biblical understanding and support.

G. Guiding people into distinguishing physical pain from pain of the spiritual heart and pursuing the appropriate help for each.

VII. There are basic categories of life whereby biblical counselors are to lead counselees through the process of putting off particular sinful habits and putting on God-honoring righteous habits.

A. Biblical counselors are to help counselees look closely at and work hard on having ***thoughts, attitudes, motives/intentions, emotions,*** and ***desires*** that are pleasing to God as God's Word commands (Rom. 12:2-3, 2 Cor. 10:3-5, 1 Cor. 4:5, Prov. 16:2, Col. 3:1-5).

B. Biblical counselors are to help counselees look closely at and work hard on ***communicating*** in ways that are honest and edifying to others as God's Word commands (Eph. 4:29).

C. Biblical counselors are to help counselees look closely at and work hard on walking in ***behavior*** that is consistent with Christ's character as God's Word commands (Eph. 4:17-32, 5:1-17, Gal. 5:16-26).

D. Biblical counselors are to help counselees look closely at and work hard on ***relating*** to others in ways that demonstrate the love of Christ as God's Word commands (Rom. 12: 9-21, 13:8-12).

E. Biblical counselors are to help counselees look closely at and work hard on ***serving*** others in ways that will bear their burdens and meet their needs as God's Word commands (Eph. 4:11-16, 1 Peter 4:10-11).

VIII. People go through *six phases* when genuine change takes place.

   A. *Realization Phase:* They come to see truth and understand how it applies to their life (2 Tim. 2:24-26).

   B. *Remorse Phase:* They feel godly sorrow in relation to their sin and desire to make things right with God and others (2 Cor. 7:10).

   C. *Renounce Phase:* They confess their sin to God and to others when appropriate (Ps. 32:1-11, Jas. 5:16).

   D. *Repentance Phase:* They turn away from their sin toward God and toward others (Prov. 28:13, 2 Cor. 7:10-11).

   E. *Renewal Phase:* They meditate on the truth so that they may learn the new direction by which they are to obey God and love others (Eph. 4:17-23).

   F. *Replacement Phase:* They obey God and love others in the area where they have disobeyed God and been unloving toward others (Eph. 4:17-23).

IX. Each *phase of change* is worked out through *stages of spiritual growth*. As God is working inside of individuals (Phil. 2:12), they respond accordingly (Phil. 2:13). Here is an example of how this process works (2 Tim. 3:16-17):

   A. **Teaching Stage:** The Holy Spirit guides, convicts, and enlightens their minds through the Word of God, the Body of Christ, circumstances, and prayer (John 16:8-13, 1 Cor. 2:9-12, Heb. 4:12, 1 John 4:4-6, 1 Peter 4:12-13, Rom. 8:26-27). (Realization Phase occurs as a result.)

   B. **Conviction Stage:** God begins to focus their attention in particular areas of life, convincing them that change is necessary (Phil. 3:14-15, 2 Cor. 7:10-11). (Realization Phase and Remorse Phase occur as a result.)

   C. **Correction Stage:** They make a decision to abandon a sin issue and begin a new thought, word, or action, trusting God's power to make things function as they should (2 Cor. 7:10-11, Prov. 28:13-14). (Renounce Phase and Repentance Phase occur as a result.)

   D. **Training Stage:** As they respond to God's conviction, they seek to put to practice what God has commanded in His Word.

1. By the power of God they walk in harmony with God in areas where they were once disobedient.

2. They are experiencing victory: a deeper fellowship with God and with others (2 Peter 1:1-11; Prov. 12:13, 24:16; John 8:31-32; Luke 8:4-18; Eph. 4:11-13; 1 John 3:1-3). (Renewal Phase and Replacement Phase occur as a result.)

X. There are several key concepts to teach within the counseling process to help counselees through each phase and stage of change.

A. *The Gospel:* The person and work of Jesus Christ for sins and salvation of mankind.

B. *What I Can and Cannot Control:* We cannot control people and the outcome of situations. We can control our own thoughts, motives, desires, words, actions, and will. Therefore, our choices reveal either our love for God and others or our selfish ambition with people and circumstances.

C. *The Two Choices in Life:* There are only two choices in life. We are either God-centered or self-centered. Our choices reveal our thoughts, and our thoughts are motivated by indwelling sin or by the Holy Spirit. When our thoughts are motivated by indwelling sin, we worship our desires, turning them into lusts of our lives. Then we look to people, places, products, and perspectives to satisfy ourselves, turning them into idols we use to satisfy our lustful desires.

D. *Idolatrous Lust:* Something we bow down to that we believe will bring us what we truly treasure, while making what we truly treasure something we bow down to in place of the living God. The *avenues* we pursue and bow down to in the form of worship (Idols) along with these *treasures* we bow down to in the form of worship (Lusts) make up the idolatrous lust in our lives.

E. *The Cycle of Relationships:* When we walk in pride we relate to people according to our picture, preferences, and presumptions, leading to pain in our hearts and the practice of treating people in unloving ways. When we walk in humility we relate to people according to their position before God and others, the priority of God for others, and the precept of God for others, resulting in peace in our hearts and the practice of love toward others.

F. *The Four Kinds of Human Relationships:* Understanding what it means to be open and unloving, closed and loving, open and loving, closed and unloving.

G. *The Biblical View of Love:* Understanding what it means to love according to 1 Cor. 13:1-8.

H. *Living by Purpose:* Understanding and developing a Christ-centered life.

I. *Conflict Resolution:* Understanding why conflict exists and how to resolve it from addressing heart issues instead of just dealing with behavior.

J. *The Biblical Framework:* Understanding what happens to a person in his heart when he chooses to sin and when he chooses to live righteously.

K. *Immaterial Pain Vs Material Pain:* Understanding that all pain is not the same. Some pain is the result of issues going in within the immaterial (non-physical) heart (soul/spirit). Some pain is the result of material issues (physical body). Some pain in the physical body happens as a result of pain within the immaterial heart. We must deal with physical pain according to medication and all that the medical world can provide. We must deal with immaterial pain according to the Messiah and all He has to provide. We should not confuse the two.

XI. There are *six* key categories of homework that can be given to guide counselees into the process of change according to each phase and stage. These projects, activities, and reading assignments can lead them into escaping the corruption of their flesh, the world, and the devil and growing into spiritual maturity in Jesus Christ.

A. *Hope Homework:* to help people gain a true hope in Christ according to the problems they are facing (Used in all stages of spiritual growth).

B. *Doctrinal Homework:* to help people gain a solid theological understanding of their problems so that they can deal with them properly (Used to lead people into the Teaching Stage of spiritual growth).

C. **Awareness Homework:** to help people become aware of their own sinfulness in the problem so that they can stop deceiving themselves about the problem they are facing and own up to it (Used to lead people into the Conviction Stage of spiritual growth).

D. **Embracing God Homework:** to help people connect with God according to a particular characteristic of God that relates to their problem or sin (Used to lead people into the Correction and Training Stage of spiritual growth).

E. **Action-Oriented Homework:** projects and activities that lead people to put off particular sinful thoughts, desires, conversations, behaviors, and lifestyles and to put on particular godly thoughts, desires, conversations, behaviors, and lifestyles, according to the situation or problem (Used to lead people into the Correction and Training Stage of Spiritual growth).

F. **Relational-Oriented Homework:** projects and activities that lead people to put off unloving relational patterns and move them to relate in open and loving relational patterns toward others (Used to lead people into the Correction and Training Stage of spiritual growth).

XII. While determining the category of homework to be given, the counselor can use various **methods** of implementation to help move counselees through each phase and stage, which can result in their escaping the corruption of their flesh, the world, and the devil and growing into spiritual maturity in Jesus Christ. Following are some of those methods of implementation.

A. **Scripture reading:** leading counselees into seeing and discovering the reality of God's Word related to their problem and into a consistent pattern of reading and studying God's Word to understand the nature of it and to live by its content. They may thus know God intimately and be useful to Him practically.

B. **Literature reading:** leading counselees into reading various biblical literature that shows them how to evaluate and address the problem from God's standpoint in a comprehensive manner, so that they may turn from it and walk in obedience to God.

C. **Scripture Memorization:** leading counselees into memorizing Scripture so that they may be transformed in their thinking and turn away from sin toward living as God has commanded.

D. *Prayer:* leading counselees into the process of prayer so they may learn how to communicate with God in a way that will lead them into genuine fellowship with God; so they may learn how to make requests for others and themselves in an appropriate manner.

E. *Projects:* activities that lead counselees into stopping some thought, word, or action or leading them into starting some thought, word, or action in relation to God, others, self, or circumstances relating to the issues brought up in the counseling sessions.

F. *Log Lists/Journals:* directing counselees to write down specific thoughts, behaviors, actions, or words to evaluate where change has taken place or to see where change needs to take place.

G. *Church Participation:* leading counselees into

   1. *Membership:* joining a local church that they may experience love and enjoy the blessings of God-honoring relationships.

   2. *Maturity:* getting involved in discipleship courses in a local church that would encourage them to love God and others on a consistent basis and living a life that reflects the character of Christ.

   3. *Magnification:* coming to appreciate, value, and adore the character of God through heart-felt genuine worship of Him in a local church.

   4. *Ministry:* joining a ministry where they can develop in bearing burdens and meeting needs according to their various relationships through the local church.

   5. *Missions:* supporting a local church in sharing and defending the Christian faith.

XIII. Overall, biblical counselors are to lead counselees into gaining a biblical understanding of

A. God and submitting to God's will.

B. Themselves and submitting to God's will.

C. Others and submitting to God's will.

D. Life's situations and circumstances and submitting to God's will.

XIV. There are four basic *kinds of counselees* counselors may see when involved in biblical counseling.

A. Those who *lack knowledge* on what to do in the situation. (Don't know what to do.)

B. Those who *have knowledge* but *lack skill* on how to apply the knowledge to their situation. (Know what to do but do not know how to do it.)

C. Those who *have knowledge* and *have skill* on how to apply the knowledge to their situation but refuse to apply what they know to the situation. (Know what to do and how to do it but refuse to do what they know.)

D. Those who *lack knowledge* and *lack skill* on how to apply the knowledge to their situation and are not interested in gaining either knowledge or skill. (Don't know what to do or how to do it and are not interested in learning either.)

XV. Counselees are ready to be released or graduated from counseling when

A. The counselees understand their problem from a biblical perspective.

B. The counselees understand the biblical solutions to their problem.

C. The counselees consistently apply the principles to address their problems to put off sin and to put on what is right, resulting in living out in practice what they have learned.

XVI. Given these factors, true biblical counseling (which in essence is evangelism and discipleship) will help people through each phase, stage, and category of life by the practice of seven key procedures (1 Thess. 5:14-24):

A. **Commend submission** (1 Thess, 5:11).

1. Congratulate counselees in areas they are seeking to do the right thing in relation to the situation.

2. Compliment counselees in areas they refused to do the wrong thing in relation to the situation.

B. **Console suffering** (Rom. 12:15).

1. Connect with the pain of the sufferer.

2. Consider the peace God can bring to the sufferer.

C. **Confront sin** (Gal. 6:1).

1. Call out sin with compassion.

2. Challenge sin with care.

D. **Characterize the Sovereign** (Col. 1:28-29).

1. Discuss the aspects of God's character that would be appropriate to consider in relation to the situation.

2. Dialogue about how those aspects of God's character can be used for warning and teach these to the person in relation to the situation.

E. **Communicate salvation** (Matt. 28:18-20).

1. Present the gospel of Jesus Christ.

2. Provide guidance for receiving the gospel of Jesus Christ.

F. **Clarify sanctification** (Matt. 28:18-20).

1. Teach the specific sins that need to be put off and how to do this through the Word of God.

2. Tutor through the Word of God the specific solutions that need to replace the specific sins and that demonstrate love for God and love for others.

G. **Celebrate summation** (Phil. 3:13-21).

1. Promote the promise of the return of Jesus Christ.

2. Proclaim the prizes that come with the return of Jesus Christ.

XVII. The following chart shows a snapshot of the big picture.

Areas of Change	Phases of Change	Stages of Spiritual Growth	Concepts to Teach in the Biblical Counseling Sessions	Homework to Help Implement Change	Methods to Help Implement the Homework	Examples of Implementing Activities	Seven Key Procedures
Thought (Idea)	Realize truth	Teaching Stage—Realize truth	The Gospel/ What I Can and Cannot Control	Hope Homework	Scripture Reading	Reading particular books of the Bible that connect to the issues	Commend Submission
Attitude (Belief System that results from a pattern of Ideas)	Realize and Remorse over our sin in connection with truth	Conviction Stage—Realize and Remorse over our sin in connection with truth	The Two Choices Concept	Theological Homework	Literature Reading	Reading literature that addresses the issues	Console Suffering
Motives or Intentions/ Emotions/ Desires	Renounce our sin	Correction Stage—Renounce our sin; Repent of our sin	Idolatrous Lust/ The Four Kinds of Human Relationships	Awareness Homework	Scripture Memorization	Memorizing and meditating on Scripture/ biblical concepts according to the issues	Confront Sin
Communication Patterns	Repent of our sin	Training Stage—Renew our minds; Replace our sin with the right thing to do in areas of change	Biblical View of Love/ Living by Purpose	Embracing God Homework	Prayer	Writing out log list, or journal to evaluate one's self or progress	Characterize Sovereign
Behavioral and Relational Patterns	Renew our minds		Conflict Resolution	Action-Oriented Homework	Projects	Communicating certain things to God or people on a regular basis	Communicate Salvation
Service for God and Others	Replace our sin with the right thing to do in areas of needed change		Biblical Framework	Relational-Oriented Homework	Log List/ Journals/ Church Participation	Practicing certain attitudes, actions, or behaviors toward God, others, and in situations / Getting involved in particular aspects of church life to enhance growth in Christ	Clarify Sanctification/ Celebrate Summation

Lessons I Have Learned in Counseling

The Three Basic Responses to People and Circumstances

Neutral Responses

Demonstrating and expressing happiness, sadness, disappointment, embarrassment, or hurt that does not violate Scripture: the normal expressions in life that God does not hold against you as wrong.

People

and

Circumstances

There are three basic responses to people and circumstances

Loving Responses

to have thoughts, motives, desires, communication patterns, behavior patterns, manner of life patterns, relationship patterns, or serving patterns we are commanded and empowered by God to have that demonstrate love for God and others.

Unloving Responses

to have unloving thoughts, motives, desires, communication patterns, behavior patterns, manner of life patterns, relationship patterns, or serving patterns that are prohibited by God and are determined by the evil in our hearts.

Four Key Issues Revealed in Our Responses to People and Circumstances

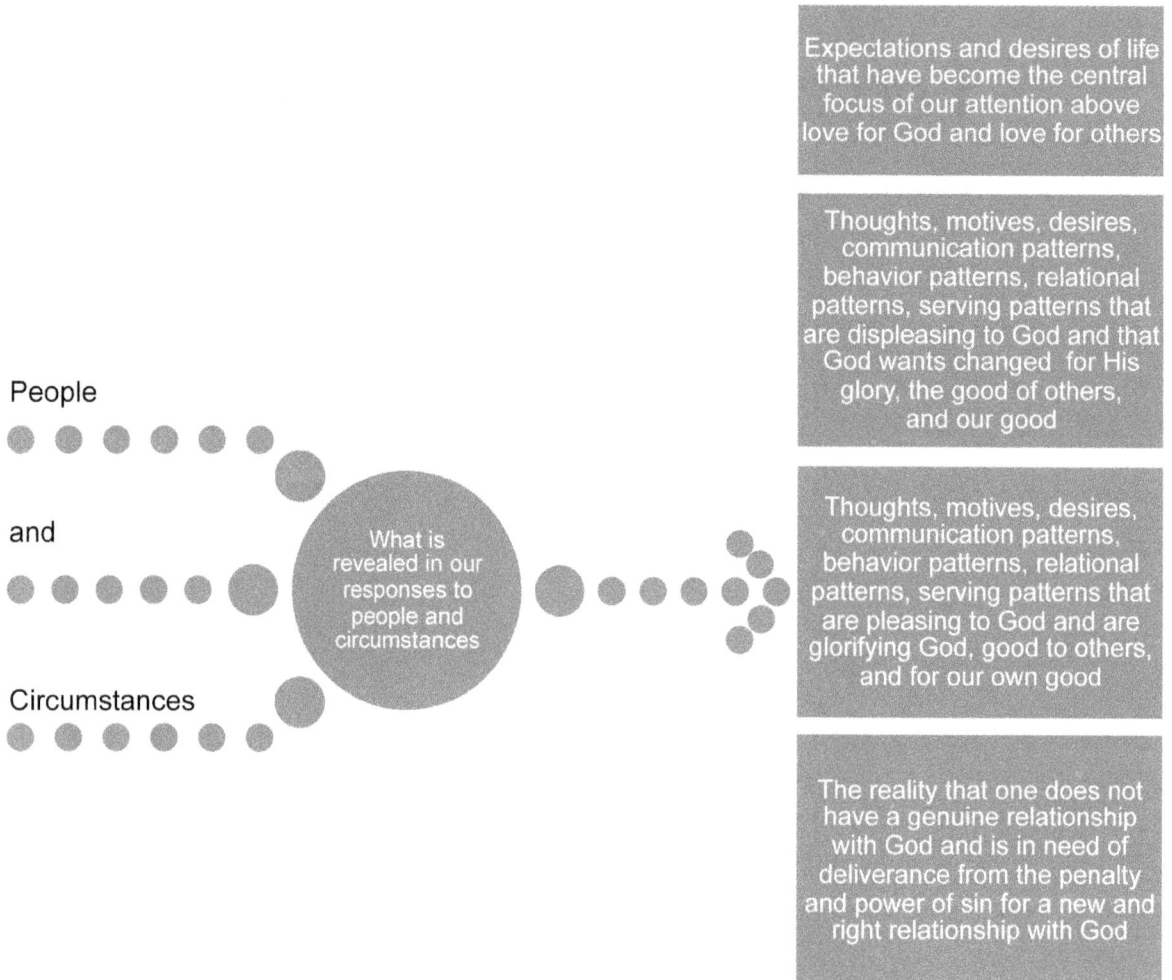

People

and

Circumstances

What is revealed in our responses to people and circumstances

Expectations and desires of life that have become the central focus of our attention above love for God and love for others

Thoughts, motives, desires, communication patterns, behavior patterns, relational patterns, serving patterns that are displeasing to God and that God wants changed for His glory, the good of others, and our good

Thoughts, motives, desires, communication patterns, behavior patterns, relational patterns, serving patterns that are pleasing to God and are glorifying God, good to others, and for our own good

The reality that one does not have a genuine relationship with God and is in need of deliverance from the penalty and power of sin for a new and right relationship with God

What I Can't and Can Control

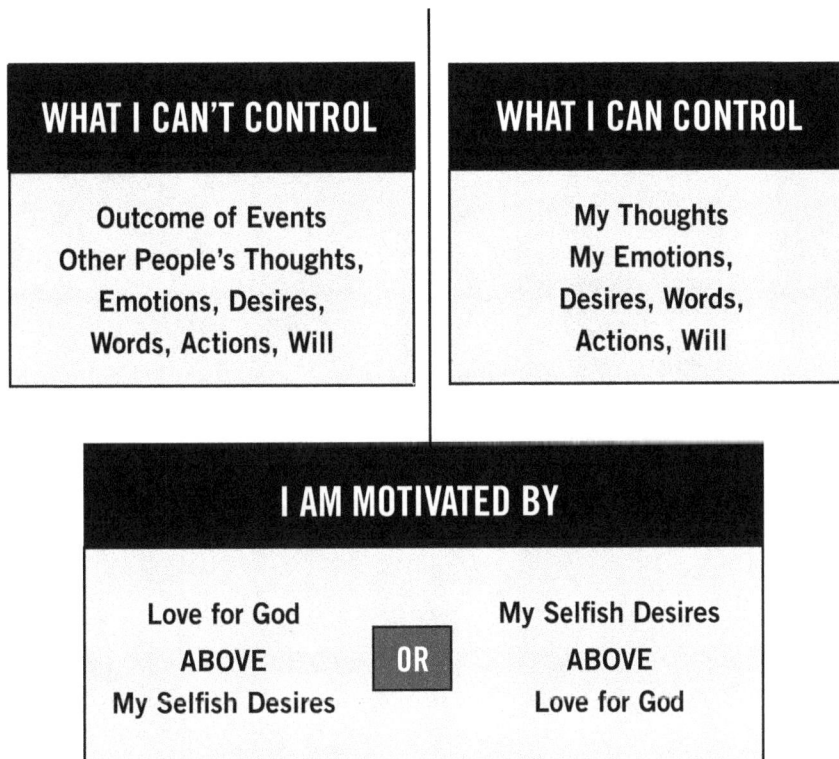

WHAT I CAN'T CONTROL

Outcome of Events
Other People's Thoughts,
Emotions, Desires,
Words, Actions, Will

WHAT I CAN CONTROL

My Thoughts
My Emotions,
Desires, Words,
Actions, Will

I AM MOTIVATED BY

Love for God
ABOVE
My Selfish Desires

OR

My Selfish Desires
ABOVE
Love for God

We cannot control people or the outcome of situations (Eccles. 3:1-11, 7:13-14, 9:1-2). We can only control our own thoughts, emotions, desires, words, and actions (Rom. 12:2-3, Prov. 16:32, Ps. 37:4, Eph. 4:29, 22-24). Therefore, we need to evaluate and take responsibility for how we are responding to people and the outcome of situations (Gal. 6:7-8, 5:16-25). We need to evaluate what is motivating us in dealing with people and the outcome of situations (Jas. 1:13-14, 3:13-16, 4:1-3). Are we motivated by love for God above our selfish desires? Or are we motivated by our selfish desires above love for God? (1 John 2:15-16, Jas. 4:4, 3:16)

Looking at Some Central Heart Issues

Pride
- Mind set on self; self-centeredness
- Life revolves around what is important to us above what is important to God. When what God says contradicts what we think, we allow what we think to be the perspective we hold above what God says. Interpret the Scripture to fit our agenda.

Lust
- Consumed with what we treasure above loving God and loving others. Willing to sin to get this treasure and to sin when we cannot receive this treasure. This treasure in essence has become an all-consuming desire that we allow to become the center of our attention above loving God and loving others

Idolatry
- Will use people, places, products, or perspectives as means to obtain or to satisfy the lust of our life. They are placed above God to satisfy the lustful desires we treasure above loving God and loving others. They are the means to our lustful end.

Worry
disturbing or disquieting thoughts of the mind as we are consumed with the possibility of losing or not receiving something we treasure

Anger
to have ungodly attitudes, words, or actions as a result of some perceived need, desire, personal preference, or standard not being met by someone or in circumstances

Depression
enslaving thought, mood, or feeling of unhappiness that becomes the reason we give for not functioning as we should

As we walk in pride, we will be consumed with lust. As we are consumed with lust, we will seek idols to satisfy our lustful desires. When the idols seemingly are not going to follow through our expectation to satisfy our lustful desires, we may begin to worry. When the idols do not follow through on our expectation to satisfy our lustful desires, we may fall into anger. All of this worry and anger could possibly lead us to depression.

As we listen and talk with people, evaluate how we are responding to other people and circumstances. Listen to the dominant topics of conversation to determine what we tend to treasure, dislike, worry about, and get angry about. Learn the people, places, products, and perspectives we tend to discuss the most and why. Listen to see if our primary conversations are driven by discussions of ourselves or others or things more important than ourselves. Identify who or what tends to lead us to react in happiness or sadness.

Direction and Result of Addressing Some Central Heart Issues

Embracing God

Entrusting ourselves to God according to the specific characteristics of God as we encounter all aspects of life.

Humility

- Mind set on Jesus Christ, God-centeredness, submission to God.
- Embracing and submitting to our roles and responsibilities in life according to God's Word.
- Life revolves around what is important to God above our desires that have become sinful and have led us into sin. When our sin-focused desires contradict what God commands, we allow what God commands to be the perspective we submit to above our sin-focused desires. We pursue God and find more pleasure in that above our sin-focused desires.

Love For God

- Consumed with following the commands of God, we are devoted to doing what God says in all aspects of life.
- Because we want to know Jesus Christ intimately, be like Jesus Christ, and be useful to Jesus Christ, we are willing and wanting to follow the commands of God--knowing obedience leads to knowing, becoming like, and being useful to Jesus Christ. We focus on doing what God says in our thoughts, motives, desires, words, actions, and way of life.
- Because God first loved us, we seek to love Him by our submission to Him in all aspects of life.

Love For Others

- Consumed with treating people with the highest level of what is called appropriate by Scripture unconditionally. Seeking the highest good of others unconditionally.
- Taking the characteristics of 1 Corinthians 13:4-8 and applying them to all unconditionally.
- Serving others unconditionally with the spiritual gifts God has given us. We become an ambassador to unbelievers and a builder of believers unconditionally.

Accepting What God Allows

Enduring the difficult, disappointing, and down times of life, knowing God is working out His ultimate good in our lives through them; Enjoying the delightful times of life, knowing God has granted them for our enjoyment and development as well; Submitting to our roles and responsibilities during the good and bad times because of our commitment to and confidence in God. Living by our commitment to God and confidence in God above our mood of the moment.

Peace of God

Tranquility of the heart as a result of embracing God and accepting what God allows in our lives. Calmness of soul regardless of the situation because of our surrender to and submission to God.

We must evaluate our lives and see where we stand. Let's identify where we lack humility, love for God and others, embracing God, accepting what God allows, and the peace of God. We then move into the process of remorse over our sin, renouncing our sin, and repenting of our sin. We recognize our pride, lust, idolatry, worry, anger (and all other sins discovered), which may have led to depression. We replace those sins with humility, love for God and others, embracing God, and accepting what God allows. We will see a difference in our lives when we start living for God and stop living for ourselves. People and circumstances will be handled by God's agenda. We will find that life is more satisfying and productive as we live to please God instead of seeking to use God, people, or circumstances to accomplish what is and has been more important to us above our allegiance to and obedience to God. We can also stop being worried or angry with God, people, or circumstances as a result of their falling short of providing what we want. We will find ourselves turning away from a life reduced to making God, people, and circumstances the help to or the complaint against us in accomplishing our personal ambitions.

As we walk in humility, we will be preoccupied with love for God and others. Living this way involves living by our commitment to God and confidence in God above our mood of the moment. As we develop in living by our commitment to God and confidence in God, we will experience the peace of God more consistently in both the good and bad of our lives.

3

The Big Picture for Biblical Counseling

I. There are only two central commands that sum up all commands:

   A. Love God

   B. Love Others

II. Man's basic problem is a lack of love of God or a lack of love of others (which is what sin is). As Christ said, "If you love me you will keep my commandments. Love your neighbor as yourself." To disobey God is to sin. To sin is to lack love for God and to lack love for others.

III. Man's lack of love for God and others shows up in five places:

   A. Thoughts, motives, desires

   B. Communicating

   C. Behavior / manner of life / conduct / commitments

   D. Relating to others

   E. Serving others

IV. We will see a lack of love for God or others in areas IIIA-E as we observe people's actions, reactions, or responses to other people and circumstances.

V. Our mission is to help people see the lack of love for God or others in areas IIIA-E and to help move them from a lack of love for God and others to walking in love for God and others.

VI. The root lack of love will be found in IIIA.

VII. The fruit lack of love will be found in IIIB-E.

VIII. We will help people understand how IIIA is driving IIIB-E.

IX. We will then lead them to walk in love for God and others in IIIA-E.

X. The tools we have to do this are the worksheets and homework assignments we give.

XI. Therefore, as we observe people's actions, reactions, or responses to other people and circumstances or listen to them talk about these issues, we should listen, identify, and document our observations on seven basic levels:

A. Level 1: The IIIA-E issues being presented or discussed.

B. Level 2: What they can and cannot control according to the issues presented or discussed.

C. Level 3: The person(s)' actions, reactions, or responses to other people and circumstances being presented or discussed.

D. Level 4: Where their actions, reactions, or responses fit on the Biblical Framework.

E. Level 5: The belief systems, agendas, and desires revealed from their actions, reactions, or responses being presented or discussed.

F. Level 6: The pride, lust, and idols revealed from their actions, reactions, or responses being presented or discussed.

G. Level 7: The IIIB-E issues that are the by-products of the IIIA issues.

XII. We will lead them to see and understand these things through the worksheets and homework we will give them.

XIII. We will lead them to renounce, repent, and replace these things with love for God and love for others through the worksheets and homework we will give them.

XIV. We will lead them to do all of this according to the person's phases and stages of change.

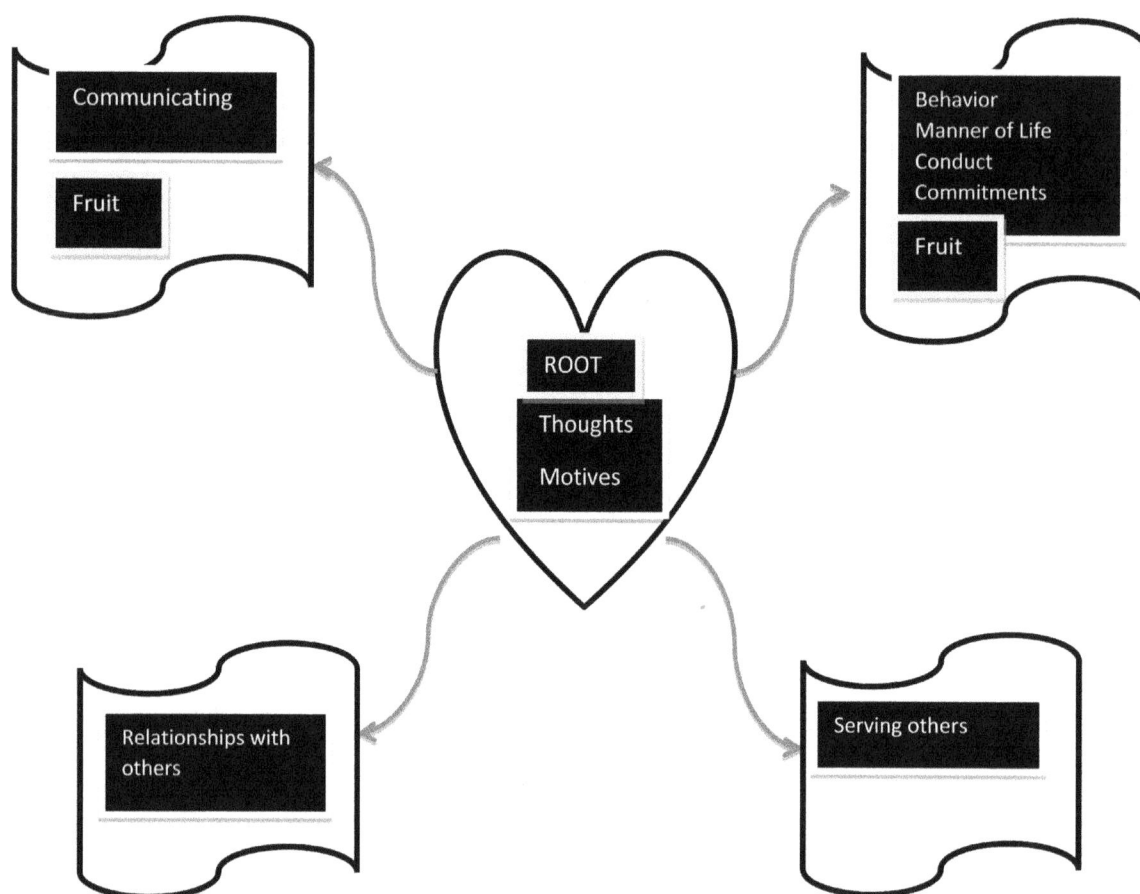

Key Point: In summary, people who come in for counseling are bringing a lot of data to us that show the <u>fruit</u> of their <u>root</u> sin. Their lack of love for God and others is sinful.

Lack of love for God: John 14:15 "If you love Me, you will keep My commands."

Lack of love for others: Mark 12:31 "The second is, Love your neighbor as yourself. There is no other command greater than these."

When gathering data, we must look beyond the "fruit" sin and stay attentive to their speech for the "root" sin. We must keep the "root" in our minds as they are communicating with us.

Luke 6:45 "A good man brings good things out of the good stored up in his heart, and an evil man brings evil things out of the evil stored up in his heart. For the mouth speaks what the heart is full of."

We must not get caught up in the "fruit" "drama" but instead ask good questions to search for the root. "What motivated you to do that?" "What were you desiring at that moment?" and so forth. If we stay in the "fruit" of the issues, we will get caught up in the "leaves" that can blind us to see the "root."

4

Policies / Consent to Counsel / Personal Data Inventory

Example of Biblical Counseling Policy

Are You Interested in Biblical Discipleship Counseling at Community of Faith Bible Church?

Biblical counselors at Community of Faith Bible Church (COFBC) are available for a limited number of counseling cases. Our counselors (by design) are not certified by the State of Texas; however, each counselor is trained and supervised by other counselors. Additionally, COFBC counselors have had extensive training in biblical discipleship counseling and must meet various training requirements established by the Bible and the Director of the Ministry.

Director of the Counseling Ministry

Dr. Nicolas Ellen, the director of the ministry, is the Senior Pastor of COFBC. In addition to his pastoral and counseling ministries at COFBC, he teaches biblical counseling at the College of Biblical Studies in Houston, Texas, in his role as Senior Professor of Biblical Counseling. He holds both M.A. and Ph.D. in Biblical Counseling. He has also written numerous books on biblical discipleship counseling and continues a national teaching ministry on the subject of biblical discipleship counseling.

The Role of Scripture to the Counselor

If you seek counseling from COFBC, we want you to know that all counseling will be conducted in accordance with the counselor's understanding of the Scriptures. All counseling will be biblically based, meaning that the Scriptures will be the authority in all cases. **COFBC does not subscribe to the teachings and methods of modern** psychology or psychiatry, whether expressly secular or the result of any attempted integration with biblical principles. **Our counselors do not follow the methods of trained or licensed psychotherapists or mental health professionals. Also, our policy is not to make referrals to such persons.**

If you (the counselee) are not sure that you will be interested in biblically based counseling, you may first attend one or two sessions to discover what biblical discipleship counseling is like. **If you or the counselor determines that you (the counselee) are unwilling to use the Bible as the final authority for your life, future counseling sessions will be terminated.**

Additionally, each counseling session will conclude with the counselor assigning homework. If the counselee is unwilling to complete the assigned homework, future counseling sessions will be terminated until the assigned homework has been completed to the satisfaction of the counselor. **Any future sessions can be terminated by either party. However, if you (the counselee) are a member of COFBC, the Pastor and/or Elders will be notified of the reasons for termination of your counseling sessions and all by-laws and/or policies of COFBC shall apply. If you are not a member of COFBC, please note that written correspondence will be sent to your church notifying them of the termination of your counseling sessions and the reasons for said termination.**

Non-members of COFBC

Please note that COFBC is committed to the spiritual health of its members, thus **counseling of COFBC members always takes precedence over all non-member-related counseling services.**

If the counselee is a member in good standing with a church other than COFBC, the counselee is **required** to invite his/her Senior Pastor, Elder, or someone else in a leadership position from his/her local church to accompany him/her to the counseling sessions.

We recognize and respect the authority and the discipline of the counselee's church. However, if no one in a leadership position is available to attend counseling sessions with the counselee, COFBC's counselor, after seeking guidance and approval from the Director of the Counseling Ministry, may decide to move forward with the counselee.

However, the counselee **must** provide to the counselor a written letter from his/her Senior Pastor and/or Elder(s) authorizing him/her to attend counseling at COFBC. This letter must be signed and on the letterhead of the counselee's church. In addition, this letter **must** provide COFBC with the name and telephone number of the person in the counselee's church who will serve as the counselee's accountability partner. We do this because we firmly believe in the leadership of the counselee's church and we only want to come alongside them to offer assistance. Also, this will make transfer back to the pastoral care of the counselee's church much easier to effect.

Additionally, if the counselee is unable to bring someone in leadership with him/her, or to provide some form of accountability from his/her local congregation, COFBC may elect not to facilitate the counseling process. This is due to the fact that COFBC believes that the Senior Pastor/Elders are responsible for the spiritual well-being of their local congregation. Without the involvement or support of the Senior Pastor/Elders or someone in leadership from the counselee's church, COFBC would be assuming responsibility for the counselee's spiritual well-being. Nevertheless, if the Director of the Counseling Ministry were to make a determination that extraordinary circumstances do exist that make this requirement unworkable, the Director of the Counseling Ministry may, at his sole discretion, elect to allow the counseling session to go forward in the absence of any approval or presence from the counselee's church leadership.

Non-member of a Church
If the counselee is currently not a member of a church, for reasons other than church discipline or unresolved sin matters, he/she will be <u>required</u> to attend Sunday services at COFBC while going through COFBC's counseling ministry. For example, if the counselee is going to have 13 counseling sessions, then COFBC would expect that the counselee would attend COFBC for 13 weeks. After such time, COFBC will be happy to assist the counselee in finding a church home and, of course, the counselee is welcome to examine Community of Faith Bible Church as a possibility.

Our experience has been that for changes in people to be lasting, people need more than the help they receive in formal counseling. They need the total ministry of a church in which the preaching, teaching, and fellowship are providing the same kind of help that is given in the counseling sessions. **If the counselee does not attend COFBC on a regular basis (i.e., Sunday services and weekly discipleship classes <u>at least three (3) times a month</u>), all future counseling sessions will be terminated.**

Confidentiality

Absolute confidentiality is not scriptural. In certain circumstances the Bible requires that facts be disclosed to select others (Matt. 18:15ff). In these areas we will follow the policy and procedures of COFBC. When a counselee's church leaders inquire about the status of his/her counseling sessions, we will disclose to them the information that is necessary for them to effectively and biblically fulfill their responsibility to shepherd the counselee.

BY LAW, there are certain situations in which information about individuals undergoing counseling may be released with or without their permission. These situations are as follows: (Romans 13:1-3)

1. Where it is proven that children are physically abused, sexually abused, or neglected.
2. In emergency situations where there may be proven danger to the counselee or others, as with homicide or suicide, confidentiality may be broken.
3. If a court of law issues a legitimate subpoena relating to a child abuse case, we are required by law to provide the information specifically described in the subpoena.
4. If an unreported life-threatening felony has been committed, we are required by law to report it to the police.

At any time during the counseling, for reasons sufficient to himself/herself, the counselor shall have the option of terminating counseling.

Counselee Responsibility

It should be understood that biblical discipleship counseling will involve giving scriptural teaching and making practical application of the same to each individual counselee. The counselee is held fully responsible for how he/she implements that counsel.

Counselors in Training

Here at Community of Faith Bible Church we not only provide biblical discipleship counseling but are devoted to training biblical counselors. This means that the counselor may have one to two people assisting him/her in each counseling session.

The Bible as the Authority in the Session

We are confident that the Bible has all of the information necessary for life and godliness (2 Peter 1:3). There are no problems between persons or in persons that the Bible fails to address either in general or specific principles. Our counselors are not infallible, nor do they pretend to know all there is to know about biblical teaching and its applications to life, but they are well equipped and competent to help people change. They will make a point to differentiate between God's commands and their suggestions. Counselors will also honestly tell you if they are limited in their capacity to address a matter and will seek help from other trained counselors in matters where they feel it is needed.

Medical/Legal Advice

Please note that COFBC does **not** give medical or legal advice.

Beginning the Biblical Counseling Process

If you are willing to enter into this kind of counseling, please fill out the forms attached below. Once you have filled out the forms please email the forms to ChurchSecretary@ cofbc.org, or mail them to us (see our contact information). Once you have emailed or mailed the forms, call us to see when/if scheduled times of counseling are available.

Thank you for your interest in the Biblical Discipleship Counseling Ministry of Community of Faith Bible Church.

Example of Consent to Counsel Policy:

Consent to Biblical Discipleship Counseling
and
Release of Liability Form

What Is Expected of You?

It is our (COFBC) belief that change must begin with ourselves as we look to Jesus Christ for the power to change. Therefore, we ask you (the counselee) to approach the counseling and encouragement process as an opportunity for personal change and spiritual growth. We ask that you refrain from the temptation of focusing on others, and instead we ask you to focus on what changes God desires to make in your life, in the midst of your circumstances. Be advised that you will be assigned "homework."

Homework is a vital part of the change process; therefore, completion of the homework assignments before your next session is expected.

CONFIDENTIALITY CLAUSE

1) Absolute confidentiality is not scriptural. **In certain circumstances the Bible requires that facts be disclosed to select others (Matthew 18:15ff). In these areas we follow the guidelines of COFBC and the Bible. When your church leadership inquires, we will disclose to them the information they need to effectively and biblically fulfill their responsibility to shepherd you.**

2) The privacy and confidentiality of our conversations and records are a privilege of yours and are protected by our ethical principles in all but a few circumstances. **BY LAW, there are certain situations in which information about individuals undergoing counseling may be released with or without their permission. These situations are as follows: (Romans 13:1-3)**

   A. Where it is proven that children are physically abused, neglected, or sexually abused;

   B. In emergency situations where it is proven that there may be danger to the counselee or others, as with homicide or suicide, confidentiality may be broken;

   C. If a court of law issues a legitimate subpoena relating to a child abuse case, we are required by law to provide the information specifically described in the subpoena;

   D. If an unreported life-threatening felony has been committed, we are required by law to report it to the police.

3) **We reserve the right to consult with others or appropriate church ministry staff members regarding your sessions.** This consultation will be held in the same level of confidence as your sessions. This will involve issues such as:

   A. Church discipline matters

   B. Seeking wise counsel to help address the matter in a thorough manner

   C. Reporting to other leaders on the status of counseling when feasible and appropriate

   D. Training of other counselors to learn how to handle cases of the same nature

Resolution of Disagreements

If a dispute should arise between the counselee and the counselor regarding the session or the counselor's advice or conduct, one should bring this dispute to the attention of the Director of the Biblical Discipleship Counseling Ministry of COFBC. If the dispute cannot be resolved at this level, all parties agree to resolve such dispute by submitting to the Conflict Resolution Team of the COFBC (which is composed of members selected by COFBC's Senior Pastor/Elders) for full and final resolution and conciliation. Both the counselee and the counselor agree NOT to take this matter to any secular court system (1 Corinthians 6:1-7).

Waiver of Liability

The undersigned counselee, having sought biblical discipleship counseling as adhered to by Community of Faith Bible Church, a nonprofit religious organization, hereby acknowledges his/her understanding of the above-stated conditions and therefore releases, acquits and forever discharges from liability the Community of Faith Bible Church, its pastor, elders, pastoral/lay counselors, members, employees, ministries, church staff, subsidiaries (including, but not limited to, Community Counseling Center), partners, agents, affiliated/participating churches and business entities, from any and all manner of actions, causes of action, suits, claims or demands in law and equity arising from out of the undersigned's participation in the above-mentioned biblical discipleship counseling ministry.

It is further understood, in consideration for receiving any form of counseling from the Community of Faith Bible Church, the person (counselee) receiving the counseling agrees to all of the provisions, terms and conditions contained within the attached Exhibit A to this Consent to Biblical Discipleship Counseling and Release of Liability Form.

The undersigned agrees that he/she has read and thoroughly understands and agrees to the terms and conditions of this Consent to Biblical Discipleship Counseling and Release of Liability Form and Exhibit A attached hereto which is incorporated by reference the same as if fully set forth herein and now willingly (without any coercion) consents to and requests said biblical discipleship counseling from COFBC's biblical discipleship counseling ministry.

SIGNED on this _____ day of _____, AD 20_____, by

Signed Name: _____

Printed Name: _____

State of Texas
County of _____

Before me, the undersigned authority on this day personally appeared _____, known to me to be the person whose name is subscribed to the foregoing instrument of writing and acknowledged to me that he/she executed the same for the purposes and consideration thereon expressed. SWORN TO AND SUBSCRIBED BEFORE ME, under my official hand and seal of office this the _____ day of _____, 20_____.

_____

NOTARY PUBLIC In and for the STATE OF TEXAS

Printed Name: _____
My Commission expires: _____

Example of Personal Data Inventory

Personal Data Inventory

Please complete this inventory carefully.

(Question marks have been omitted.)

PERSONAL IDENTIFICATION:

Name _____ Birth Date _____

Address _____ Zip _____

Age _____ Sex _____ Referred By _____

Marital Status:

Single ___ Engaged ___ Married ___ Separated ___ Divorced ___ Widowed ___

Education (last year completed): _____

Home/Cell Phone _____ Business Phone

Employer _____ Position _____ Years _____

In case of emergency, please contact: _____(name)

_____(Phone numbers)

MARRIAGE AND FAMILY:

Spouse _____ Birth Date _____

Age _____ Occupation _____ How long employed _____

Home/Cell Phone _____ Business Phone _____

Date of Marriage _____ Length of dating _____

Give brief statement of circumstances of meeting and dating _____

_____

Have either of you been previously married _____ To Whom _____

Have you ever been separated _____ Filed for divorce _____

Information about children:

Name	Age	Sex	Living	Yrs. Ed.	Step-child

Describe relationship to your father _____

Describe relationship to your mother _____

Number of siblings _____ Your sibling order _____

Did you live with anyone other than parents _____

Are your parents living _____ Do they live locally _____

HEALTH

Describe your health _____

Do you have any chronic conditions _____ what _____

List important illnesses and injuries or handicaps _____

Date last medical exam _____ Report _____

Physician's name and address _____

Current medication(s) and dosage _____

Have you ever used drugs for other than medical purposes _____

If yes, please explain _____

Have you ever been arrested _____

Do you drink alcoholic beverages _____ If so, how frequently and how much _____

_____

Do you drink coffee _____ How much _____

Other caffeine drinks _____ How much _____

Do you smoke _____ What _____ Frequency _____

Have you ever had interpersonal problems on the job _____

_____

Have you ever had a severe emotional upset _____ If yes, explain _____

_____

Have you ever seen a psychiatrist or counselor _____ If yes, explain _____

_____

Are you willing to sign a release of information form so that your counselor may write

for social, psychiatric, or other medical records _____

SPIRITUAL:

Denominational preference _____

Church attending _____

Church attendance per month (circle one) 0 1 2 3 4 5 6 7 8+

Do you believe in God _____ Do you pray _____

Would you say you are a Christian or still in the process of becoming a Christian _____

_____

Have you been baptized _____

How often do you read the Bible Never _____ Occasionally _____ Daily _____

Explain any recent changes in your religious life _____

_____

WOMEN ONLY:

Have you had any menstrual difficulties _____ If you experience tension, tendency to cry, other symptoms prior to your cycle, please explain _____

Is your husband willing to come for counseling _____

Is he in favor of your coming _____ If no, explain _____

PROBLEM CHECKLIST:

___ Anger	___ Depression	___ Loneliness
___ Anxiety	___ Drunkenness	___ Lust
___ Apathy	___ Envy	___ Memory
___ Appetite	___ Fear	___ Moodiness
___ Bitterness	___ Finances	___ Perfectionism
___ Change in lifestyle	___ Gluttony	___ Rebellion
___ Children	___ Guilt	___ Sex
___ Communication	___ Health	___ Sleep
___ Conflict (fights)	___ Homosexuality	___ Spousal abuse
___ Deception	___ Impotence	___ A vice
___ Decision-making	___ In-laws	___ Other

BRIEFLY ANSWER THE FOLLOWING QUESTIONS:

1. What is the problem or concern that brings you here today? _____

_____

_____

_____

_____

_____

_____

2. What have you done about this problem?

_____

_____

_____

_____

_____

_____

3. What are your expectations from counseling?

_____

_____

_____

_____

_____

_____

_____

4. Is there any other information we should know about?

_____

_____

_____

_____

_____

_____

PERSONAL INVENTORY: Matthew 7:1-5

Rate yourself on each of the following traits. Before each word, put the number from the rating scale which most accurately describes you.

Rating Scale: 0 = Never   1 = Seldom   2 = Sometimes   3 = Often   4 = Usually

_____ Loving	_____ Courteous
_____ Honest	_____ Creative
_____ Sensitive	_____ Decisive
_____ Good father/mother	_____ Efficient
_____ Works hard	_____ Forgiving
_____ Humble	_____ Generous
_____ Keeps his/her word	_____ Frugal
_____ Dependable	_____ Appreciative
_____ Does not take advantage	_____ Hospitable
_____ Does not use people	_____ Diligent
_____ Not an opportunist	_____ Discerning
_____ Plans ahead	_____ Encouraging
_____ Knows where he/she is going	_____ Enthusiastic
_____ Fair	_____ Courageous
_____ Consistent	_____ Conscientious
_____ Perseveres	_____ Patient
_____ Admits it when wrong	_____ Considerate
_____ Teachable	_____ Persistent
_____ Analytical	_____ Punctual
_____ Compassionate	_____ Disciplined
_____ Cooperative	_____ Resourceful
_____ Neat	_____ Sincere
_____ Objective	_____ Other

SPIRITUAL CONVICTIONS QUESTIONNAIRE: (Please use the back of this sheet if necessary.)

1. Describe who God is: _____

_____

_____

2. Describe who Jesus Christ is: _____

_____

_____

_____

_____

_____

3. Describe the kind of relationship you have with God and His Son Jesus Christ: _____

_____

_____

_____

4. What is the definition of a Christian?

_____

_____

_____

_____

5. I am or (I am not) a Christian because: _____

_____

_____

_____

6. What do you believe about the Bible?

_____

_____

_____

_____

_____

7. What is your definition of sin?

_____

_____

_____

_____

8. What sins do you struggle with the most?

_____

_____

_____

_____

9. How do you handle sin in your life?

_____

_____

_____

_____

10. How do you handle guilt?

_____

_____

_____

_____

11. What do you tend to pray about the most?

_____

_____

_____

_____

12. What do you seek to accomplish in life?

_____

_____

_____

_____

13. I do attend or I do not attend church because: _____

_____

_____

_____

14. I allow Christians or I do not allow Christians to be involved in my life because: ___

_____

_____

_____

15. The changes I would like to make in my life are _____

_____

_____

_____

_____

16. What have you learned about yourself and what have you learned about your partner? What changes do you need to make in light of filling out this form? _____

_____

_____

_____

_____

_____

The Eight Cs of Biblical Counseling / The Initial Counseling Session

The Eight Cs of Biblical Counseling

I. **Connect** with the counselee in the first part of the counseling session.

    A. Ask your counselee questions that will help you to get to know her/him better.

    B. Identify areas of common interest and share those with the counselee.

    C. Share things about yourself that you think will lead your counselee to be comfortable with you (Prov. 16:24).

II. **Console** the counselee during the counseling session.

    A. Give words of hope and encouragement to assure the counselee that God has solutions to his/her problems.

    B. Provide comfort as the counselee shares his/her problems and concerns.

    C. Be compassionate and patient as the counselee shares his/her heart with you.

III. **Collect** data from the counselee about her/his problems and concerns.

    A. Find out what is happening or has happened to the person.

    B. Identify what she/he cannot control, what she/he can control, the motives (God-centered or self-centered) that are being revealed in her/his choices or responses to the people/circumstances.

    C. Find out how she/he is responding in thoughts, words, behavior, lifestyle, relational patterns to what is happening or has happened (neutral, unloving, loving responses).

    D. Identify time frame of responses to people, places, events in accordance to what is happening or has happened.

    E. Find out what she/he wants that she/he cannot control getting and what she/he is getting that she/he does not want.

    F. Identify areas of pride, idolatrous lust, worry, anger, fear, depression.

    G. Find out what the person's perceptions, preferences, pains, passions are in connection to what is happening or has happened.

    H. Find out how the person has dealt with or is dealing with sin toward God and others.

    I. Look for any and all unloving thoughts, words, and actions.

IV. **Categorize** data from the counselee into biblical terms and perspectives as you are thinking through biblical solutions.

    A. What are the IIIA-E issues being revealed in the situation?

    B. What can he/she control and cannot control?

    C. What are the neutral, loving, and unloving responses in the situation?

    D. In what phase or stage is this person, in light of dealing with the situation?

    E. Is this a salvation issue?

    F. Is this a suffering issue?

G. Is this a sin/sanctification issue?

H. Is this a sage issue?

I. Is this a soma issue?

J. Is his/her pride, idolatrous lust, anger, worry, or depression being revealed in the situation?

V. ***Communicate*** to the counselee what the Bible defines as the source and the symptoms of the problems in biblical terms and ***clarify*** what the biblical solutions are to those problems. Explain the following concepts.

A. The gospel.

B. What I cannot and can control.

C. The biblical framework.

D. The point of choice.

E. Pride.

F. Idolatrous lust.

G. Worry, anger, fear.

H. The cycle of relationships.

I. Four kinds of human relationships.

J. Love for God and others.

K. Progressive sanctification.

L. Confession, repentance, and replacement.

M. The material and immaterial (nonphysical) aspects of man.

N. Guilt and the standards of the conscience.

O. The fear of man, anxiety, and the solutions.

P. Embracing God according to who He is.

Q. Being controlled by the Holy Spirit.

VI. **Challenge** the counselee to a commitment to confess, repent, and replace sin with love for God and others.

   A. Ask the counselee if he/she is willing to do the hard work of confessing, repenting, radically amputating, and replacing sin to walk in love for God and others.

   B. Explain to the counselee the importance of being a doer of the Word and not just a hearer of the Word.

   C. Explain what kind of commitment it will take to make the appropriate changes to resolve the problem and become godly in the situation.

VII. **Construct** homework for the counselee to apply to his/her life that will lead him/her into confession, repentance, and replacement of sin with love for God and others.

   A. *Hope Homework:* projects, activities, and reading assignments given to help people gain a true hope in Christ related to the problems they are facing.

   B. *Doctrinal Homework:* projects, activities, and reading assignments given to help people gain a solid theological understanding of their problems so that they can deal with them properly.

   C. *Awareness Homework:* projects, activities, and reading assignments given to help people become aware of their own sinfulness in the problem so that they can stop deceiving themselves about the problem they are facing and own up to it.

   D. *Embracing God Homework:* projects, activities, and reading assignments given to help people connect with God according to a particular characteristic of God that relates to their problem or sin.

   E. *Action-Oriented Homework:* projects and activities that lead people to put off particular sinful thoughts, desires, conversations, behaviors, and lifestyles and to put on particular godly thoughts, desires, conversations, behaviors, and lifestyles related to the situation or problem.

F. *Relational-Orientated Homework:* projects and activities that lead people to put off unloving relational patterns and move them to relate in open and loving relational patterns toward others.

VIII. ***Conjoin*** the counselee to the Body of Christ according to where she/he needs it.

A. *Membership:* the counselee would be led to join a local church so that she/he may experience love and enjoy the blessings of God-honoring relationships.

B. *Maturity:* the counselee would be led to get involved in discipleship courses in a local church that would lead her/him into loving God, loving others on a consistent basis, and living a life that reflects the character of Christ.

C. *Magnification:* the counselee would be led to come to appreciate, value, and adore the character of God through heart-felt, genuine worship of Him in a local church.

D. *Ministry:* the counselee would be led to join a ministry where she/he can develop in bearing burdens and meeting needs according to the various relationships she/he will develop through the local church.

E. *Missions:* the counselee would be led into supporting a local church in sharing and defending the Christian faith.

The Initial Counseling Session

I. **Connect** with the counselee in the first part of the counseling session.

   A. Ask your counselee questions that will help you to get to know him/her better.

   B. Identify areas of common interest and share those with the counselee.

   C. Share things about yourself that you think will lead your counselee to be comfortable with you (Prov. 16:24).

II. **Collect** data from the counselee in regards to his/her problems and concerns.

   A. Find out what is happening or has happened to the person.

   B. Identify what he/she cannot control, what he/she can control, the motives (God-centered or self-centered) that are being revealed in his/her choices or responses to the people/circumstances.

   C. Find out how he/she is responding in thoughts, words, behaviors, lifestyle, relational patterns to what is happening or has happened (neutral, unloving, loving responses).

   D. Identify time frame of responses to people, places, events in accordance to what is happening or has happened.

   E. Find out what he/she wants that he/she cannot control getting and what he/she is getting that he/she does not want.

   F. Identify areas of pride, idolatrous lust, worry, anger, fear, depression.

   G. Find out what the person's perceptions, preferences, pains, passions are in connection to what is happening or has happened.

   H. Find out how the person has dealt with or is dealing with sin toward God and others.

   I. Look for any and all unloving thoughts, words, and actions.

III. **Categorize** data from the counselee into biblical terms and perspectives as you are thinking through biblical solutions.

   A. What are the IIIA-E issues being revealed in the situation?

   B. What can she/he control and cannot control?

   C. What are the neutral, loving, and unloving responses in the situation?

   D. In what phase or stage is this person, in light of dealing with the situation?

   E. Is this a salvation issue?

   F. Is this a suffering issue?

   G. Is this a sin/sanctification issue?

   H. Is this a sage issue?

   I. Is this a soma issue?

   J. Is her/his pride, idolatrous lust, anger, worry, or depression being revealed in the situation?

IV. **Console** the counselee during the counseling session.

   A. Give words of hope and encouragement to assure the counselee that God has solutions to her/his problems.

   B. Provide comfort as the counselee shares her/his problems and concerns.

   C. Be compassionate and patient as your counselee shares her/his heart with you.

V. **Clarify** the direction and what is expected from the counselee if he or she is willing to meet for more sessions.

   A. Communicate to the counselee the process of how you will provide biblical counseling as it relates to times, dates, structure, etc.

   B. Communicate to the counselee the need to be faithful, available, and teachable.

C. Communicate to the counselee the importance of doing his/her homework and doing it thoroughly.

D. Communicate to the counselee the importance of being willing to *grow* through the process and not just *go* through the process.

E. Communicate to the counselee that the goal will not be to make counseling work to fit his or her personal agendas but to work through counseling to conform to God's agenda.

F. Ask if he/she is interested in coming back; if so, give him/her homework of meditating on a verse that you used in consoling him/her.

VI. **Consider** what the primary issues(s) is/are and follow the counseling process accordingly.

A. Salvation Issues

B. Suffering Issues

C. Sin/Sanctification Issues

D. Soma Issues

E. Sage Issues

6

The Cul-De-Sacs of Life / Tracks of Counseling

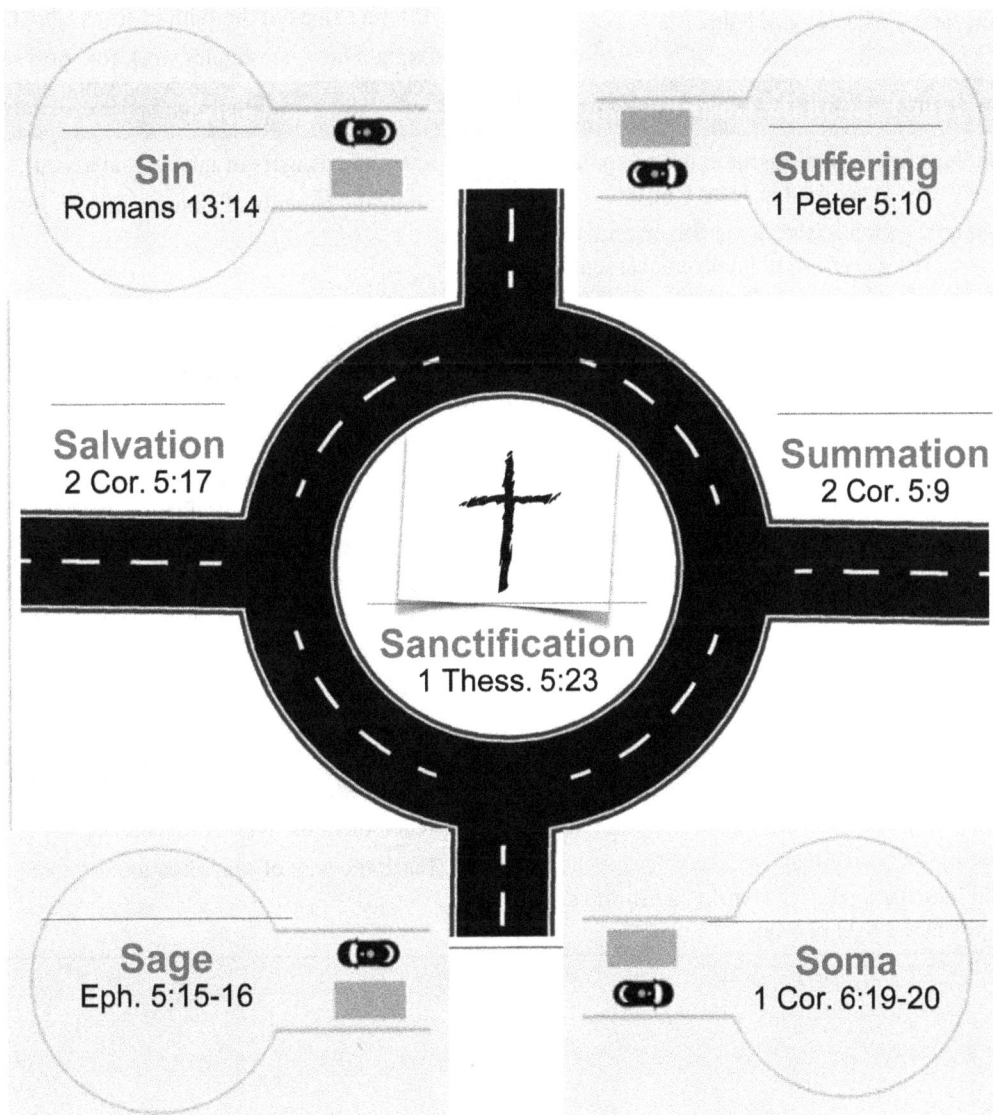

Sin
Romans 13:14

Suffering
1 Peter 5:10

Salvation
2 Cor. 5:17

Summation
2 Cor. 5:9

Sanctification
1 Thess. 5:23

Sage
Eph. 5:15-16

Soma
1 Cor. 6:19-20

Salvation Concepts to Teach

Concept 1 – The Gospel of Jesus Christ

- Teach who Jesus Christ is.
- Teach the doctrine of salvation.

- Teach the way of salvation.
- Teach the evidence that validates one has received salvation.

Concept 2 – Understanding the Difference Between Faith That Works and Working for Salvation

- Explain Paul's Theology of Faith.
- Explain James' Theology of Faith

- Show how Paul and James are explaining different sides of the faith in Jesus Christ.
- Explain how one cannot work for one's salvation.

Concept 3 – True Faith in the Gospel Vs Intellectual Awareness of the Gospel

- Explain how intellectual assent to the person and work of Christ is not trust in Jesus Christ.
- Explain how genuine faith in the person and work of Jesus Christ goes beyond intellectual assent to putting trust in what one understands.

- Show the dangers of intellectual assent.
- Show the benefits of genuine faith in Jesus Christ.

Concept 4 – From Salvation to Sanctification to Satisfaction

- Explain how we were saved from the penalty, power, and soon presence of sin.
- Explain how we are saved unto sanctification into the image of Jesus Christ.

- Explain how sanctification will lead to satisfaction as we obey God.
- Explain how Psalm 16:11 applies to the salvation, sanctification, and satisfaction experience.

Concept 5 – Spiritual Deception

- Teach people the danger of practicing religion.
- Teach people how easy it is to be deceived into thinking they are Christians due to some acts of ministry service when actually they are not.

- Help people examine themselves to see if they are deceived about being a Christian.
- Lead them into faith if they have been deceived.

Concept 6 – Spiritual Amnesia

- Explain how some Christians have forgotten the purpose of their salvation.
- Explain how the light of the world has dimmed their eyes to the light of God.

- Teach them the way of repentance.
- Teach the way of sanctification.

Suffering Concepts to Teach

Concept 1 – Emotions

- Define emotions from the Latin—which means to stir up one to actions.
- Explain and demonstrate how emotions come from thoughts of the mind and brain.
- Explain and demonstrate how emotions operate.
- Help individuals connect the teaching to their lives accordingly.

Concept 2 – Understanding and Dealing with Suffering

- Teach and explain the definition of suffering—to experience pain or distress as a result of choices within our control and choices beyond our control.
- Teach and explain why we suffer—sin, sanctification, or Satan.
- Teach and explain how to think about suffering.
- Teach and explain how to deal with suffering.

Concept 3 – Kinds of Sorrow

- Teach and explain common sorrow—a sadness of the soul due to one's experiencing the disappointments of life, the difficulties of life, or the death of a loved one.
- Teach and explain chosen sorrow—a sadness of the soul created by grumbling or complaining about one's circumstances.
- Teach and explain conscience sorrow—a sadness of soul as a result of one's conscience bringing about guilt due to some act(s) of sin in one's life.
- Teach and explain casualty sorrow—a sadness of soul as result of regret over the consequences of sin choices, ultimately leading one to death because of a lack of repentance.
- Teach and explain contrite sorrow—a sadness of soul because one is broken over one's sin against God.
- Teach and explain chastisement sorrow—a sadness of soul because one is experiencing the discipline of God leading to a product of righteousness in one's living.

Concept 4 – How To Deal With the Past

- Help people identify what they did not want from the past that they still think about with revenge, anger, fear, or worry in the present and repent of it.
- Help people identify what they lost or did not receive in the past that they still treasure in their hearts in selfish, self-centered ways in the present and repent of it.
- Help people identify past sinful actions and decisions that have caused present-day problems and lead them to repent of it.
- Help people interpret their past and live in the present by the will of God.

Sin / Sanctification (Moving Through Awareness / Brokenness / Change Process)

Concept 1 – What I Cannot and Can Control

- Teach the person to distinguish between what one is concerned about and what one is responsible for.
- Help the person understand how not making the distinction can create complications resulting in one's negating one's responsibilities by being consumed with what one is concerned about but cannot control.
- Help the person understand that one cannot control what people think, say, or do.
- Help the person understand that one cannot control the outcome of events.

- Teach the person that one can control what one thinks, says, does.
- Help the person understand that one is motivated either by selfish desires or love for God in relation to people and situations.
- Help the person understand that the condition of one's life is a by-product of heart choices, not the actions of others or circumstances in life.

Concept 2 – The Point of Choice

- Teach the person that one is either God-centered or self-centered.
- Teach the person that one's choices are driven by one's thoughts.
- Teach the person that at the core of one's thoughts is either the love of self and the love of pleasure or the love of God and the love of others.

- Help the person understand that if one is consumed with the love of pleasure and the love of self, one may create idols and lust in one's heart and bring destruction to one's life as a result.
- Teach the person the steps to turn from this sin and all other sinful ways and turn to God.

Concept 3 – The Biblical Framework

- Help the person understand that our ambition in life is to please God.
- Help the person understand that God has given us two basic commandments to please Him (Love God and Love our neighbor).
- Teach the person that God has set up consequences within our hearts to happen when we don't walk in love for God and love for others.
- Teach the person that God has set up consequences within our hearts to happen when we walk in love for God and love for others.

- Help the person learn and understand the principle and picture of a sense of guilt, apparently uncaused fear, and apparently uncaused fleeing as the consequences of not walking in love for God and others.
- Help the person learn and understand the principle and picture of the peace of God, confidence before God, and drawing near to God as the consequences of walking in love for God and others.
- Help the person learn and understand the process of moving from a lack of love for God and others to love for God and others.

Concept 4 – Pride	
• Explain that pride is ultimately a self-centered way of living. • Give examples of pride.	• Help the person learn how pride operates in one's life. • Lead the person to repent of pride.

Concept 5 – Idolatrous Lust	
• Teach the concept of idols. • Give examples of idols. • Teach the concept of lust. • Give examples of lust.	• Explain the term Idolatrous Lust. • Give demonstrations of how idols are used to gain lustful desires of one's heart. • Help the person identify the idolatrous lusts of his/her heart. • Lead the person to repentance and embracing God.

Concept 6 – Worry	
• Define worry—the fear of not getting something you want or need, the fear losing something you want or need, or the fear of getting something you don't want or need as a result of being consumed and controlled by these things that are very important to you from this world below and in this world below. • Help people see that worry is an attitude that moves into emotions, causing us to be negatively preoccupied with what may or may not happen.	• Lead people into understanding that the driving force behind worry is the desires that have become demands that one has the potential to lose or gain, resulting in one's responding in worry to the future potential. • Lead people to repent and embrace God.

Concept 7 – Anger	
• Define anger—a disposition of the mind that entertains antagonism toward others, resulting in various emotions and actions. • Help people see that anger is an attitude that moves into emotions and then expresses itself in various actions.	• Lead people into understanding that the driving force behind anger is the desires that have become demands that are not being satisfied, resulting in one's response in anger to unmet desires that have become demands. • Lead people to repent and embrace God.

Concept 8 – Sorrow and Repentance	
• Teach the categories of worldly sorrow and godly sorrow. • Have the person identify the kind of sorrow he or she is experiencing.	• Teach the practice of repentance. • Lead the person into the practice of repentance.

Concept 9 – The Purpose of Life	
• Explain the glory of God. • Teach the principles of knowing God, becoming like God, and being useful to God.	• Teach the principle of learning, living, and loving by the truth. • Teach the person about being a disciple, ambassador, and builder for God.
Concept 10 – The First and Greatest Commandment	
• Teach various ways God loves us. • Teach what it means to love God.	• Teach specific areas of life where one can love God. • Help individuals learn how to put this into practice. • Teach how to embrace God.
Concept 11 – The Second and Great Commandment	
• Teach the basic categories of Love. • Teach the calling to Agape Love.	• Teach the characteristics of agape love. • Help people understand how it applies to their life.
Concept 12 – Living by Purpose	
• Teach and explain a biblical view of God and His agenda. • Help people lay out a mission plan for their life and family according to God's agenda.	• Help people identify the God-given roles and responsibilities for themselves and family and write out a job descriptions of each according to Scripture. • Help people organize their life around these particular roles and responsibilities in a way that is God-honoring.

Soma Issues

Concept 1 – Is Medication Okay For Christians?	
• Teach the nature of man as being material/immaterial glory. • Teach the reality of pain as being both physical and immaterial.	• Teach the reality of medication being effective for physical problems. • Teach the reality of medication being a wonderful support but terrible solution for immaterial pain.
Concept 2 – A Biblical Perspective on Illness	
• Explain the origin of illness. • Explain the key perspective to teach people struggling with physical illness.	• Explain an approach to help people with physical illness.
Concept 3 – A Biblical View of Psychotropic Drugs	
• Explain why Christians may be on psychotropic drugs. • Present a biblical perspective on psychotropic drugs.	• Provide an approach on how to help Christians on psychotropic drugs.

Sage

Concept 1 – Understanding Foolishness	
• Explain three categories of foolishness. • Explain various characteristics of foolishness.	• Explain seven ways to address foolishness.
Concept 2 – Understanding Wisdom	
• Explain the definition of wisdom. • Teach the difference between the wisdom of God and the wisdom of the world.	• Teach and explain how to gain and keep the wisdom of God. • Describe the characteristics of people who have the wisdom of God. • Teach and explain the benefits of gaining the wisdom of God.

Relationship Principles to Teach
(Continuation of Sin / Sanctification)

Concept 1 – Why Do We Need Relationships?

- Teach and explain how people were created for God's glory.
- Teach and explain that we need relationships to help us be productive for God.

- Teach and explain how we need relationships to help us when we fall into various troubles.
- Teach and explain how we need relationships to help us resist various temptations we face.

Concept 2 – The Cycle of Relationships

- Explain the picture, preference, and presumption of a relationship.
- Explain the pain and practice of a relationship.

- Explain the position, priority, and precepts of a relationship.
- Explain the peace and practice of a relationship.

Concept 3 – The Four Kinds of Human Relationships

- Explain the principle of being open and unloving—right insight but mean in presentation.
- Explain the principle of being closed and loving—have the desire to give truth and be beneficial to others but lack the time or ability to present it.

- Explain the principle of being open and loving—right insight and kind in approach; providing what is beneficial to others.
- Explain the principle of being closed and unloving—having bitterness in heart toward others but acting as if one is okay with others.

Concept 4 – Biblical View of Friendship

- Teach and explain the definition of friendship—one who is intimately close to another in a productive, God-honoring way.
- Teach and explain how a good friend is first a friend of God.

- Teach and explain the various practices of a godly friend.
- Teach and explain the problems that can ruin a godly friendship.

Concept 5 – Biblical View of Dating

- Teach and explain the 1 Timothy 5:1 principle.
- Help singles learn how to be brothers and sisters and not lovers.

- Help singles move from friendship to engagement to marriage.
- Help them determine not to do anything on a date that they would have to stop doing if either of them were married to someone else.

Concept 6 – The Categories of Conversations

- Explain the preference principle of conversation—conversations based on opinions.
- Explain the wisdom principle of conversation—conversations based on learning the best course of actions.

- Explain the conscience principle of conversation—conversations based on personal, acquired standards.
- Explain the moral principle of conversation—conversations based on what is right and wrong according to Scripture.

Concept 7 – Conflict Resolution

- Teach the source of conflict—lustful desires.
- Teach the steps it will take to identify the lustful desires that are creating the conflict.

- Lay out the steps it will take to seek forgiveness from the parties involved within the conflict.
- Lay out the plan to identify the associated problems and the solutions needed for problems.

Concept 8 – The Fear of Man

- Help people understand what it means to be afraid of man.
- Help people understand the danger of respecting man as they should respect God.

- Help people understand what it means to depend on man as a source of life.
- Help people understand what it means to fear being exposed, rejected, physically hurt or oppressed, or being denied what we desire.

Concept 9 – Forgiveness

- Teach the definition of forgiveness—to disregard, to let go, to release from, to pardon, to cancel a debt owed.
- Teach the person how to forgive.

- Teach the person the danger of not forgiving.
- Teach the person the difference between love and forgiveness.

Concept 10 – Hypercriticism

- Define hypercriticism—being irritated with and very critical of someone else who has the very same issues you have, while denying that fact in your own life.
- Teach people how to identify hypercriticism.

- Help people work through the very issues they are criticizing in others.
- Help people serve others in their issues after they deal with those issues in their own life.

Practical Issues to Consider Teaching
(Continuation of Sin / Sanctification)

Concept 1 – The Conscience

- Explain the definition of the conscience.
- Explain the categories the conscience uses to judge.
- Explain why there is no such thing as false guilt.
- Help people apply this to their lives.

Concept 2 – Self-Esteem, Self-Image, and Self Love

- Teach and explain Self-Esteem—satisfaction or dissatisfaction with one's self according to one's choice to live right or wrong.
- Teach and explain Self-Image—understanding of who one is or not, one's identity, and Self Love.
- Teach and explain Self Love—regard for one's self on a right and wrong level.
- Explain how Self-Esteem, Self-Image, and Self-Love work together.

Concept 3 – The Six Rs of Change

- Teach and explain what it means to realize—to be aware of the truth.
- Teach and explain what it means to be remorseful—to be convicted of the sin in connection with the truth.
- Teach and explain what it means to renounce—to confess your sin.
- Teach and explain what it means to repent—to turn away from sin.
- Teach and explain what it means to renew—to meditate on the truth in which one is to walk to replace the sin.
- Teach and explain what it means to replace—to put into practice the truth that overrides the sin.

Concept 4 – Understanding and Dealing with Temptations

- Teach and explain the definition of temptation—an enticement presented to lead one into sin against God.
- Teach and explain about the lusts of our hearts.
- Teach and explain how lusts of our hearts are the very things that the devil uses against us by providing opportunities for us to satisfy those lusts.
- Teach and explain the signs and the solutions for temptation.

Concept 5 – The Blessings of Disappointed Expectations

- Teach and explain why we have disappointments.
- Teach and explain how disappointments can reveal the sin issues of our hearts.
- Teach and explain how disappointments can lead us to deal with the sin issues of our hearts.
- Help people learn to handle disappointments in a God-honoring way.

DYNAMICS OF BIBLICAL COUNSELING

Concept 6 – Learning To Be Content	
• Define contentment—satisfaction within the soul apart from people and circumstances as a result of fellowship with God. • Evaluate the Apostle Paul and identify his journey to contentment.	• Teach and explain the various Scriptures on contentment. • Help people develop a track to move toward contentment.
Concept 7 – Decision-Making in the Will of God	
• Teach people about the sovereign will of God. • Teach people about the moral will of God.	• Teach people about the non-moral will of God. • Help people learn how to make decisions according to the concepts above.
Concept 8 – Humility	
• Teach the definition of humility—a mind set on Christ with submission to the will of God. • Give examples of humility.	• Help people learn where humility needs to take place. • Help people learn how to walk in humility.

Sample of Data Gathering / Case Report Form

Name of Counselee

Date:

Session #1

1. Main issue(s) presented in session (C stands for category):

C1 Thought, belief systems, intentions, agendas, motives, desires, emotions:

C2 Communication Patterns:

C3 Behavior/ Manner of Life Patterns:

C4 Relational Patterns:

C5 Serving Patterns:

2. Significant thoughts revealed by counselee in session:

3. Category of issue presented by counselee:

Suffering issue:

Salvation issue:

Sin/Sanctification issue:

Soma issue:

Sage issue:

4. What he/she can control in light of issue(s) presented by counselee / significant thoughts revealed by counselee:

5. What he/she cannot control in light of issue(s) presented by counselee / significant thoughts revealed by counselee:

6. Responses to people / circumstances in light of the issue(s) presented by counselee / significant thoughts revealed by counselee:

Neutral:

Loving:

Unloving:

7. Heart issues being revealed in light of the issue(s) presented by counselee / significant thoughts revealed by counselee:

Prideful Belief Systems:

Motives / Agendas / Intentions:

Emotions demonstrated and revealing:

Lust: _____ Idol: _____

Anger:

Worry:

Any other heart issues:

8. What phase/stage is the counselee in with problem(s) presented by counselee / significant thoughts revealed by counselee in session (circle which one applies):

Phase: Realization, Remorse, Renounce, Renew, Repent, Replace

Stage: Teaching, Conviction, Correction, Training

9. What are the current responses of the people involved with counselee and the current status of the situation in light of the previous counseling session (to be answered after session 1)?

10. Key insights you shared with the counselee in light of issue(s) presented by counselee / significant thoughts revealed by counselee in current session:

    Worksheet:

    Scriptures:

    Pamphlet:

    Audio:

    Video:

    Etc.:

11. Key homework given to counselee in light of issue(s) presented by counselee / significant thoughts revealed by counselee in current session:

    Doctrinal:

    Awareness:

    Hope:

    Embracing God:

    Action-Oriented:

    Relation-Oriented:

12. Into what phase/stage do you need to guide the counselee in light of this counseling session? (Circle which one applies)

Phase: Realization, Remorse, Renounce, Renew, Repent, Replace

Stage: Teaching, Conviction, Correction, Training

13. What key insights do you need to share in the next counseling session in light of this counseling session?

Worksheet:

Scriptures:

Pamphlet:

Audio:

Video:

Etc.:

14. What homework do you need to give in the next counseling session in light of this counseling session?

Doctrinal:

Awareness:

Hope:

Embracing God:

Action Oriented:

8

When Encouragement Is Not Enough

Key Point: Encouragement is not designed for people who are unmotivated or unwilling to perform a task or are suffering at the hands of other people and/or circumstances. Therefore, it will not be enough in those situations and will not work. We must learn when and how to give the counsel and support of practical encouragement.

I. How do we define the counsel and support of encouragement?

A. To guide or come alongside people in order to strengthen, to inwardly calm, to stir up or motivate them to perform an action or task.

B. To guide or come alongside people in order to fill with courage or strength of purpose, especially in preparation for a hard task. (Deut. 1:38, 3:28; 2 Chron. 35:2; Is. 35:3; Acts 11:23, 14:22; Rom. 15:5; 1 Cor. 16:12; Col. 2:2; Titus 2:4; Heb. 3:13, 10:25; 1 Thess. 2:11, 3:2, 5:11, 5:14)

II. When is encouragement not enough?

A. Encouragement is not designed for people who are unmotivated and/or unwilling to perform a task. Therefore, encouragement is not enough and will not work.

B. Encouragement is not designed for people who are suffering at the hands of other people and/or circumstances. Therefore, encouragement is not enough and will not work.

III. What do we do with people who are unmotivated and/or unwilling to perform a task?

A. People who are unmotivated and/or unwilling to perform a task need the counsel and support of correction.

B. The counsel and support of correction can be defined as providing guidance or coming alongside people to confront them to confess and repent of their sin; to challenge, correct, mold, or perfect the mental faculties or moral character so that people function in the way intended; to provide guidance or come alongside people to help them get back to operating within their God-given roles and responsibilities by any God-honoring insight and action that is appropriate. (Deut. 8:5; Job 5:17; Prov. 13:1, 15:32, 19:20; Heb. 12:9-11; Gal. 6:1-2)

IV. What do we do with people who are suffering at the hands of other people or circumstances?

A. People who are suffering at the hands of other people need the counsel and support of consolation.

B. The counsel and support of consolation can be defined as providing guidance or coming alongside people to provide empathy and support in order to help them endure hardships of suffering from people and/or circumstances; to guide or come alongside people in order to help alleviate the grief, sense of loss, or trouble they are encountering through people and/or circumstances. (Job 42:11; Ps. 94:19; Jer. 16:5; John 11:19, 31; 1 Cor. 14:3)

V. How do we discern when to give the counsel and support of correction, consolation, or encouragement?

A. As you listen to the person, identify if he/she is suffering from other people and/or circumstances. If so, then provide the counsel and support of consolation.

B. As you listen to the person, identify if he/she is sinning against God, people, and in circumstances, resulting in being rebellious against doing the action or task he/she is commanded to do. If so, then provide the counsel and support of correction.

C. As you listen to the person, identify if he/she is wanting to do something, ready to do something but has apprehension, uncertainty, lack of knowledge, or lack of skill. If so, then provide the counsel and support of encouragement according to what is needed.

VI. How do we provide the counsel and support of encouragement?

A. We can offer "The Counsel of Clarification"—guiding people in what they are supposed to do, in order to motivate or move them to do a task or action, i.e., clarifying the point of practice.

B. We can offer "The Counsel of Cultivation"—guiding people into how to do what they are supposed to do, in order to motivate or move them to do a task or action, i.e., cultivating the act of practicing.

C. We can offer "The Counsel of Calculation"—guiding people into understanding the value and importance of why they should do something and the consequences of not doing it, in order to motivate or move them to do a task or action, i.e., counting the cost.

D. We can offer "The Counsel of Cheer"—providing supporting, motivational, or inspirational words to motivate or move people to do a task or action, i.e., cheering them in the act of practicing.

E. We can offer "The Commitment to Coming Alongside"—providing some kind of action or service of support and/or cheer, in order to motivate or move people to do a task or action, i.e., coming alongside them in words or actions in the act of practicing.

Summary: Trying to encourage someone unmotivated and/or unwilling to perform a task will not work. Trying to encourage someone suffering at the hands of other people and/or circumstances will not work. This is why telling people to "Cheer up—

it will get better" or sharing Bible verses or sharing your struggles and how you made it through may seem to fall flat. You are offering the counsel of encouragement where the counsel and support of consolation or correction may need to take place. We see in Scripture that encouragement is designed to nudge people forward who are on the brink of performing some task that lies immediately in front of them when they have some uncertainty or some apprehension in performing the task.

9

Biblical Hope

Definition of Hope: Expectation of a desired outcome

I. Hope that comes from God will *not disappoint* us (Rom. 5:1-5).

A. This hope is *provided* by God's grace to us (Rom. 5:1-2).

B. This hope is *produced* through tribulation, perseverance, and developed character (Rom. 5:3-4).

C. This hope is *promoted* by the Holy Spirit (Rom. 5:5).

II. Hope that comes from man's opinions will *deceive* us (Prov. 16:25).

A. False hope is *built* on human ideas (Prov. 14:12).

   1. All my problems would be solved if I had a better job.

   2. If I could have who and what I want in life, I would be happy.

   3. If my husband/wife would just give me my way, I would be happy and all my problems would be solved.

B. False hope is *based* on an improper interpretation of Scripture (2 Peter 3:14-18).

   1. Since God owns it all, I should never be without.

   2. Since God is my Father, I should be healed of all diseases.

   3. God will give me anything I want if I just ask for it.

   4. We should call those things that are not as though they are.

C. False hope is **_birthed_** by the passions of ungodly men (2 Peter 2:1-3).

    1. If I treat people right, I will not be mistreated by others.

    2. If I can believe it, then I can achieve it.

    3. There is a perfect mate for everyone.

    4. If I serve others, surely they will return the favor and serve me.

III. Hope that comes from God will _draw_ us near to God (Heb. 7:11-19).

A. This hope **_drives_** us to depend on Christ (Heb. 7:11-19).

    1. We can expect God never to leave us or forsake us (Heb. 13:5-6).

    2. We can expect God to be our help in time of need (Heb. 4:14-16).

    3. We can expect God to help us make it through every trial and temptation we face (1 Cor. 10:13).

    4. We can expect God to provide all we need according to His riches in glory in Christ Jesus (Phil. 4:19).

B. This hope **_develops_** stability in our faith (Heb. 6:13-19).

    1. Because we have been saved we can expect to live in heaven with Jesus (John 14:1-4).

    2. Because we have been saved we can expect to receive a glorified body like Jesus Christ (Phil. 3:20-21).

    3. Because we have been saved we can expect God to perfect the things concerning us (Ps. 138:8).

C. This hope **_deepens_** our confidence in Christ (Phil. 1:12-21).

    1. We can expect God to work all things together for our good (Rom. 8:28).

    2. We can expect God to do exceedingly abundantly more than all we could ever ask or think (Eph. 3:20).

    3. We can expect God to order our steps (Ps. 37:23).

IV. Hope that comes from God will *direct* us to the return of Christ (1 John 3:1-3).

A. This hope leads us to *focus* on Christ and His glory (Titus 2:11-14).

B. This hope leads us to *favor* the blessings we will receive at His return (1 Peter 1:13).

C. This hope leads us to *forsake* our sin so we can be like Christ (1 John 3:1-3).

V. You must take time to *discern* the kind of the hope that lies within you.

A. *Examine* your life and see what your hope is placed in.

B. *Consider* who or what you are depending on to bring it to pass.

C. *Determine* if what you are hoping for is promised to you by God.

VI. You must take time to develop in the hope that comes from God (Heb. 12:1-3).

A. *Identify* what false hopes you have been trusting in.

B. *Consider* the specific promises of God you need to hope in and replace the false hopes you have been trusting in.

C. *Replace* those false hopes you have been trusting in with specific promises of God.

A Biblical Perspective on Emotions

I. Definition of *Emotion*

A. The word originated from the Latin *emovere* (*e-*, "out" plus *movere*, "move").

B. It means to "stir up."

C. Stirrings move one to actions or decisions.

II. The World's View of Emotions

A. The world sees emotions as a product of man's evolutionary history.

B. Emotions are viewed as unwilled thoughts and reactions to circumstances that are predetermined by biological processes of the body.

C. Emotions are seen as originating out of the physical body.

III. The Biblical View of Emotions

A. The Bible demonstrates that emotions have their origin in immaterial (non-physical) aspects of human nature, demonstrating that humans are created in the image of God.

B. God is Spirit (John 4:24) and has no physical brain or body. In His very nature He possesses qualities that are consistently regarded by human wisdom as emotions. Examples: Love (1 John 4:8, 16), Jealousy (Nahum 1:2), Anger (Heb. 3:10), Hatred (Ps. 5:5), Joy (1 Tim. 1:11), Sorrow (Eph. 4:30).

C. Not only does God possess emotions apart from a material existence, His Word also teaches that He has created humans in His own image (Gen. 1:26) with an immaterial aspect to human nature in which men and woman also experience emotion. Examples: Godly or sinful hatred (Ps. 105:25, Lev. 19:17), Anger (Eccl. 7:9, 11:10), Envy (Prov. 23:17), Fear (John 14:27, Deut. 28:17, Isa. 35:4), Joy (Ps. 13:5, John 16:22), Sorrow (John 16:6, Rom. 9:2).

D. Emotions from a biblical perspective can be described as sensations of the soul that occur as a result of the thoughts and attitudes of the mind thereby also exposing the values, desires, and motivations associated with those thoughts and attitudes of the mind.

E. "In a sense, emotions are the empirical evidence of the soul's existence and its executive control over the body" (Berger, *Rethinking Depression*, 173).

IV. God's Judgment of Emotions

A. Emotions of animals originate in their brains and bodies, and they have no immaterial nature in which they are responsible to God.

B. Humans, on the other hand, have an immaterial nature, and according to Scripture, most of her or his emotions originate in that nature.

C. God weighs as right or wrong those moral attitudes in man's life which determine the emotions. God does not judge the experience of the emotions themselves as right or wrong, but He does weigh the heart attitudes which initiate them (I Cor. 4:5, Jer. 17:10, Heb. 4:12).

D. Emotions prove or demonstrate that humans have a value/moral system within the fabric of their immaterial nature.

V. The Three Areas Where Emotions Originate

A. *Attitude*—Human emotions originate as a thought or a system of thoughts in a person's immaterial heart which then are experienced as sensations in his/

her immaterial heart, physical brain, and physical body. Examples: Grief (Matt. 26:36-38), Disappointment (Prov. 13:12), Agony (Luke 22:44).

B. *Conscience*—Human emotions originate as thoughts of warnings or affirmations of the conscience upon a person's right or wrong attitudes, words, and actions. The conscience excuses or accuses her/him (Rom. 2:14-15), which in turn stimulates the sensations she/he experiences in her/his immaterial heart, physical brain, and physical body from the excusing and accusing of the conscience. Examples: Bothered conscience (1 Sam. 24:5), Troubled conscience (2 Sam. 24:10), Confidence (1 John 3:21).

C. *Physiological*—Human emotions originate in a person's material brain as thoughts or warnings of possible physical danger or thoughts of pain or pleasure being experienced as sensations in the body connected to the physical nerve endings. Examples: Startle or Fright (Ruth 3:8), Pleasure (Prov. 21:17), Affliction (2 Cor. 4:8).

Emotions

God is Spirit; He has emotions.
We are created in His image.

Since we are created in His image, our emotions mainly come from our immaterial heart.

Our thoughts/attitudes determine what we feel; they determine our emotions.

Therefore, our emotions are a by-product of our thoughts/attitudes.

These emotions derive from three areas:

a. A person's mind produces attitudes that produce emotions.

b. The conscience produces attitudes (right or wrong) that produce emotions.

c. The brain produces warnings, resulting in the emotions of startle or fright as well as pleasure or pain.

Since emotions come from our immaterial heart—

There is no such thing as damaged emotions, because emotions are the window to the thoughts and attitudes of our hearts.

We cannot be emotionally abused by others, because our emotions/feelings are a by-product of what we are thinking. We decide what we will think, which determines our emotions/feelings.

We control our emotions by controlling our thoughts/attitudes because emotions come from what we are thinking. If we control our thinking we control our emotions/feelings.

No one can determine what we feel because our feelings/emotions come from our thoughts/attitudes. Therefore, no one hurts our feelings. We have feelings/emotions of hurt because of what we are thinking about the person who disappointed us or sinned against us.

As a result, we cannot blame anyone for our feelings/emotions. The way we choose to think determines the way we feel or the emotions we have.

VI. Examples of each of these kinds of emotions

A. Attitude Emotions

1. *Neutral Attitude Emotions:* common joy, common sorrow, amusement, delight, ecstasy, elation, enjoyment, euphoria, happiness, grief, anguish of heart, discomfort, displeasure, distress (when distress simply means troubled, not hopeless), loneliness (when the reference is to one's relationship with other people), sadness, sorrow, uneasiness, unhappiness, embarrassment, regret

2. *Moral Attitude Emotions:* benevolence, contentment, empathy, gratitude, love, pity, sympathy, aggression, agitation (where it does not simply mean physical discomfort), anger, annoyance, fury, hate, hostility, irritation, rage, vexation, anxiety, apprehension, distress (when this means worry and is not physically referenced), dread, fear, terror, worry, dejection, depression, gloom, hopelessness (which is not only a Moral Attitude Emotion but is also a Conscience-Stimulated Attitude Emotion to be discussed later), envy, jealousy, contempt, pride, self-pity, ungratefulness, thanklessness, passivity, submission, confidence

3. *Situational Moral Attitude Emotions* (neutral attitude emotions that are used in a loving or unloving way): taking *pleasure* in wickedness, *rejoicing* in the suffering of the wicked, rejoicing in the repentance of sin, grief over not being able to sin as you want

B. Conscience Emotions

1. the sense of guilt, the sense of apparently uncaused fear (fear of judgment, bothered or troubled conscience)

2. the sense of peace, the sense of confidence before God

C. Physiological Emotions

1. startled, frightened, bodily pain

2. bodily pleasure

VII. The role a counselor should allow a counselee's emotions to play in counseling.

    A. Counseling should evaluate the emotions being presented by others as a means to determine the attitudes of a counselee's heart. Since we know that emotions stem from attitudes, the key would be to learn the attitude to change through evaluating the emotions being presented.

    B. One can tell the difference between sinful emotions and righteous emotions. Sinful emotions in essence are sinful attitudes being displayed through the emotion. Righteous emotions in essence are righteous attitudes being displayed through the emotion. Therefore, we evaluate the emotion according to character of it. (See VI.)

    C. The counselor can use Scripture to help a counselee change improper emotions. Identify the attitude that is determining the emotion. Then lead the person to realize, be remorseful, renounce, and repent of the sinful attitude behind the emotion. Finally, lead the person to renew his or her mind in the right attitude and then replace the sinful attitude with the right attitude leading to the resulting proper emotions.

Understanding and Working through Suffering and Sorrow

Dealing with Suffering in Our Lives

I. Definition of _Suffering_: to experience pain or distress as the result of choices within our control and choices beyond our control.

The Origin of Suffering

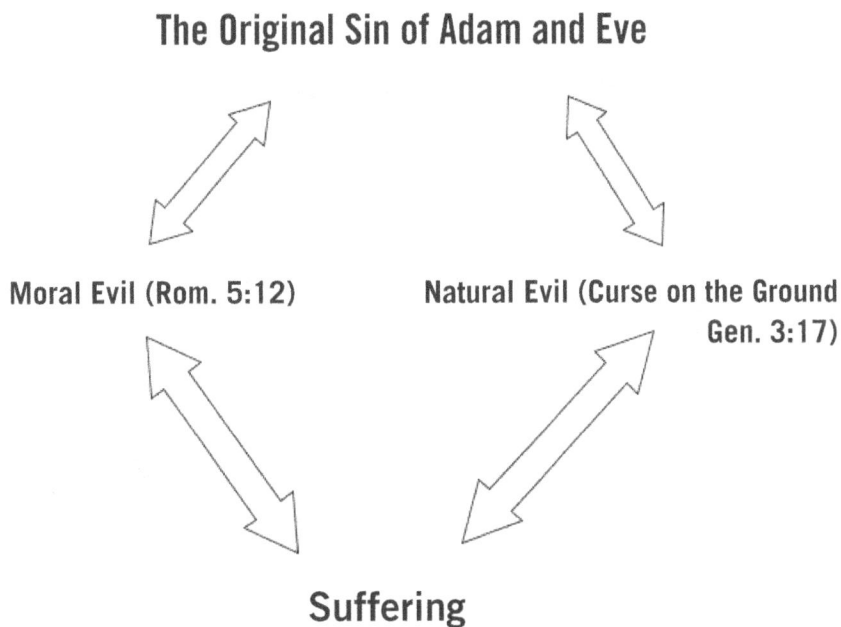

The Original Sin of Adam and Eve

Moral Evil (Rom. 5:12)   Natural Evil (Curse on the Ground Gen. 3:17)

Suffering

II. Twelve Basic Causal Categories of Suffering

A. Sometimes we suffer because of *soil evil*: God's curse on the ground as a result of Adam and Eve's sin, resulting in all sorts of natural disasters (Gen. 3:17, Rom. 8:20-22, Job 1:19). (The creation was subjected to futility; hence great winds struck the homes of Job's children, leading to their death.)

B. Sometimes we suffer as a result of *situational evil*: malfunction of manmade items. (Luke 13:4-5). (Eighteen died from the tower in Siloam falling on them.)

C. Sometimes we suffer as a result of *sickness*: physical ailments and issues that limit or cause discomfort in the natural movement and function of the body (Matt. 9:12).

D. Sometimes we suffer as a result of the *sin of self*: disobedience to God in all aspects of life (Gal. 6:7-8, Ps. 38:1-18). (Walking in the flesh brings corruption; the unrepentance of David led to suffering in the flesh.)

E. Sometimes we suffer as a result of the *sin of others*: disobedience of others resulting in negative consequences in your life (Ps. 119:161, 1 Sam. 26:17-25). (David was persecuted by Saul.)

F. Sometimes we suffer as a result of *Satan*: the enemy seeking to kill, steal, and destroy (Luke 22:31). (Satan sought to sift Peter, not to bless him but to hurt him.)

G. Sometimes we suffer as a result of coming to *salvation*: the flesh, the world, and the devil seeking to keep one from embracing the salvation of Jesus Christ through some sort of pain or distress (1 Thess. 1:5-7). (The Thessalonians received the word in much tribulation.)

H. Sometimes we suffer as a result of pursuing *sanctification*: pain or distress that has come to motivate biblical change or as a result of biblical change (Heb. 12:11, 1 Peter 4:1-3). (No discipline seems joyful but after one is trained from it, one develops in righteousness. As one seeks to walk in what is right, one will suffer in the flesh.)

I. Sometimes we suffer as a result of *serving*: being used by God as a vessel of honor to be productive for the advancement of His Kingdom in all aspects (2

Tim. 4:14-15, Matt. 5:11-12). (Alexander the coppersmith did much harm to Paul as Paul was serving God. You are blessed when insulted, persecuted, or someone falsely accuses you as a result of serving Jesus Christ.)

J. Sometimes we suffer to keep us from *self-importance*: to keep us from exalting ourselves, we may suffer some form of pain (2 Cor. 12:7). (Because Paul was given so much revelation, God sent a messenger of Satan to torment him, a thorn in the flesh to keep him from exalting himself.)

K. Sometimes we suffer to discover and demonstrate the *soundness of our faith*: going through various kinds of trials and tribulations so that we may see how strong or weak our faith is in Christ our King and to change or to continue in that faith, resulting in receiving the prize of our faith (1 Peter 1:5-9). (Saints were suffering through various trials, and their faith demonstrated love, belief, and rejoicing.)

L. Sometimes we suffer as result of God *snipping* us: God may prune our character to make us more productive in bearing fruit for Him (John 15:2). (God pruned the disciples that they might bear more fruit for the Kingdom of God.)

III. The Right Perspective to Consider When Suffering

A. We must embrace the fact that God is in *control* of all suffering (Eccles. 7:13-14, 9:1).

B. We must embrace the fact that we will *not escape* from the experience of suffering in this lifetime (John 16:33).

C. We must embrace the fact that God has already undergone the *worst* of all suffering on our behalf (2 Cor. 5:21, 1 Peter 2:21-25).

D. We must embrace the fact that God the Son and God the Holy Spirit are praying on behalf of individuals who *belong* through Jesus Christ to God the Father (Rom. 8:26-27, Heb. 7:23-25).

E. We must embrace the fact that God will bring *good* (transformation of character into the image of Jesus Christ) out of suffering for the individuals who belong to Jesus Christ (Rom. 8:28-32).

F. We must embrace the fact that God will bring *comfort* to the people who are His and are suffering as a result of seeking to serve for God's will and good pleasure (2 Cor. 1:1-7).

G. We must embrace the fact that God will bring the people who are His *through* the suffering they encounter (1 Peter 5:10-11).

H. We must embrace the fact that God will inflict more *suffering* on the people who belong to Him when they refuse to turn away from practicing the sin that is currently bringing suffering to their lives (1 Cor. 11:27-32).

IV. The Right Response to Suffering

A. If we are suffering from *soil evil* and *situational evil*, we should seek to worship God as we grieve our suffering, accepting the sovereignty of God over our lives while working through the matter with endurance. We must pursue wisdom to fix, resolve, or work through the matter and seek support from fellow Christians (Job 1:19-20, Eccles. 7:13-14, 9:1; Jas. 1:1-5, Rom. 12:15).

B. If we are suffering from *sickness*, we should pray for help, repent if there is any sin tied to the sickness, trust in the Lord, and function in obedience in spite of our sickness (Jas. 5:13-15, Prov. 3:5-8). And in all feasible situations, we can seek medical support.

C. If we are suffering from the *sin of self*, we should renounce our sin, repent of our sin, renew our minds in the truth, and replace our sin with right living to restore the joy and peace to our lives (Prov. 28:13-14; Ps. 51:1-19, 32:1-11).

D. If we are suffering from the *sin of others*, we should embrace the reality that what others meant for evil, God will use to bring good to our lives while we obey God in spite of the sin of others. Where appropriate, we should confront them about the sin (Gen. 50:12, Rom. 8:28, Rom. 12:17-21, Luke 17:3, Gal. 6:1).

E. If we are suffering from *Satan's attack* to be kept from *self-importance*, we should submit to God and resist the devil with the spiritual armor given to us by God, which will cause the devil to flee from us (Jas. 4:7, Eph. 6:13-17).

F. If we are suffering from receiving *salvation* because others do not want us to change, we should become an example to others as we serve God and wait for the return of Jesus Christ (1 Thess. 1:6-10).

G. If we are suffering from *sanctification* or to demonstrate the *soundness of our faith*, we should endure and persevere, anticipating the perfect result of our sanctification and of sound faith, which is our transformation into the image of Jesus Christ, and focus on the hope to be realized in Christ Jesus our Lord (Jas. 1:1-5, Rom. 8:28-29, Rom. 5:1-5).

H. If we are suffering from *serving* or from the *snipping of God*, we should embrace the fact that God will provide comfort in the midst of our affliction while we continue to serve. This will result in developing in endurance and Christ-like character (2 Cor. 1:1-7, Jas. 1:1-4).

Dealing with Sorrow in Our Lives

I. *Common* Sorrow (Prov. 13:12, Job 1:13-22, 1 Peter 2:19, John 11:30-35, Rom. 12:15) – a sadness of the soul due to experiencing the disappointments of life, the difficulties of life, or the death of a loved one. For example:

A. We have a sadness of heart as a result of unmet expectations, yet there is no corresponding sin with that sadness.

B. We have a sadness of heart as a result of experiencing tragedy or being mis-treated by others, yet there is no corresponding sin with that sadness.

C. We have a sadness of heart as a result of experiencing the death of someone we cared about, yet there is no corresponding sin with that sadness.

Response: We are to embrace the sovereignty, wisdom, and love of God in this sorrow as we go through this sorrow. The goal is not to hinder or stop this sorrow but to accept that God has our best interest at heart and will use it to His glory and our good overall.

II. *Chosen* Sorrow (Ex. 16:7-8, Num. 14:1-2)—a sadness of the soul created by our grumbling or complaining about our circumstances. For example:

A. We do not like and are unwilling to accept what God has allowed in the circumstances, so we complain about it, creating a sadness of soul.

B. We are unwilling to accept that people are not operating as we would like them to, so we complain about it, creating a sadness of soul.

C. We unwilling to accept the difficulties in life, so we complain about it, creating a sadness of soul.

Response: We are to repent of the unloving attitudes and actions and embrace the sovereignty, wisdom, and love of God. We are to accept what God has allowed while submitting to what He has commanded.

III. *Conscience* Sorrow (Rom. 2:14-15, 1 Sam. 24:1-5, 2 Sam. 24:10)—a sadness of soul as a result of our conscience bringing about guilt due to some act(s) of sin in our lives. For example:

A. We have been thinking in a sinful manner.

B. We have been talking in a sinful manner.

C. We have been living in a sinful manner.

Response: We are to repent of the unloving attitudes and actions and embrace the sovereignty, wisdom, and love of God. We are to accept what God has allowed while submitting to what He has commanded.

IV. *Casualty* Sorrow (Gen. 4:1-14, 2 Cor. 7:10)—a sadness of soul as result of regret over the consequences of sin choices, ultimately leading us to death because of a lack of repentance. For example:

A. We are sorrowful about what is going to happen to us as a result of the sin.

B. We are not focused on how our sin has dishonored God or damaged others.

C. Since there is no change of heart and only grief about the issue, we experience more complications, problems, pain, and ultimately death because of the consequences of a continued life of sin.

Response: We are to repent of the unloving attitudes and actions and embrace the sovereignty, wisdom, and love of God. We are to accept what God has allowed while submitting to what He has commanded.

V. *Contrite* **Sorrow (2 Cor. 7:10-11, Luke 18:9-14)**—a sadness of soul because we are broken over our sin against God. For example:

A. We are grieved over how our sin has dishonored God.

B. We are grieved over how we have brought sorrow to God because of our sin.

C. As a result of grief over sin against God, we want to and move toward making things right with God according to God's will and ways.

Response: We are to repent of the unloving attitudes and actions and embrace the sovereignty, wisdom, and love of God. We are to accept what God has allowed while submitting to what He has commanded accordingly.

VI. *Chastisement* **Sorrow (Heb. 12:11)**—a sadness of soul because we are experiencing the discipline of God, leading to a product of righteousness in our living. For example:

A. We are grieved as we experience the discipline of God, producing righteousness in our thoughts, desires, and motives.

B. We are grieved as we experience the discipline of God, producing righteousness in our communication, behavior, manner of life, or manner of serving.

C. We are grieved as we experience the discipline of God, producing righteousness in our relationship patterns.

Response: We are to endure the pain and accept what God is allowing, while submitting to what He has commanded.

VII. Essential Practices to Consider with Sorrow

A. Grieve the disappointment, death, difficulties, devastation, denial, damage, or distance that has happened.

B. Accept what God has allowed and surrender to the reality of God's will within the context of the sorrow.

C. Confess and repent of any and all unloving thoughts, desires, words, or actions.

D. Identify the attribute of God most needed for us to depend on in light of our sorrow and embrace it by faith.

E. Adjust our desires to fit the situation; accept what we cannot have and have lost in the situation, while embracing what we can have and can continue to glean and gain from the situation.

F. Identify the specific commands of Scripture that apply to our situation and seek to apply them accordingly.

Key Point: God uses sorrow in our lives. God controls the sorrow in our lives. We must trust God's love and learn how to handle sorrow accordingly. We can choose to rely upon self and false hopes and be crushed in our spirit as a result, when handling sorrow. Or we can choose to depend on God to go through and grow through our sorrow, resulting in a heart of gladness. For the Christian, sorrow is never separated from the realities of his or her character deficiencies and the need to develop in Christ-like character and fellowship with God through the sorrow. How people respond to sorrow depends upon their relationship to God, their treasures, their hopes, their view of human nature, and in whom and in what they place their identities.

12

What You Cannot and Can Control

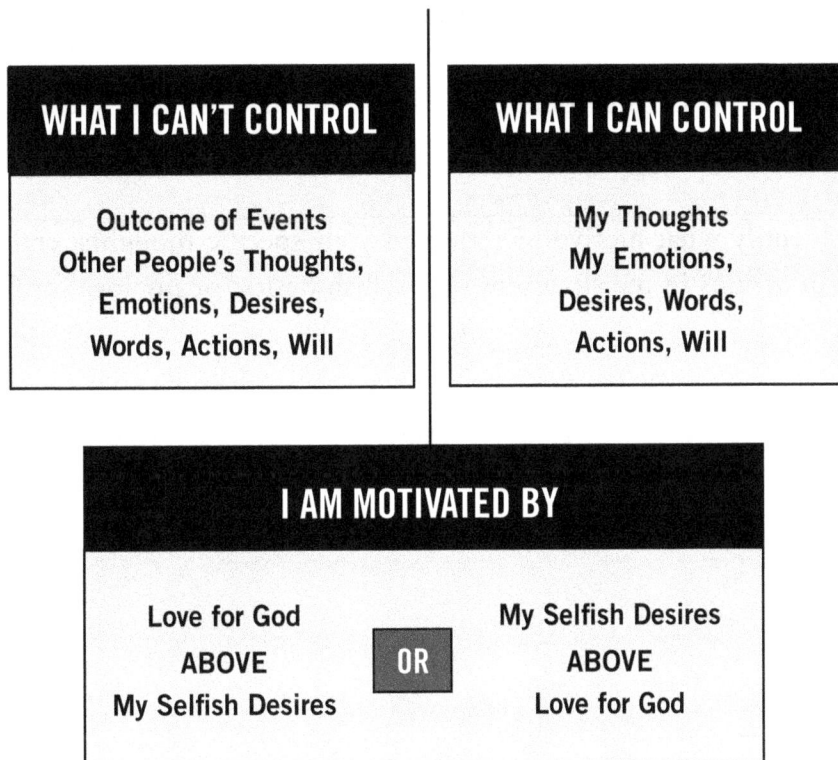

WHAT I CAN'T CONTROL	WHAT I CAN CONTROL
Outcome of Events Other People's Thoughts, Emotions, Desires, Words, Actions, Will	My Thoughts My Emotions, Desires, Words, Actions, Will

I AM MOTIVATED BY

Love for God
ABOVE
My Selfish Desires

OR

My Selfish Desires
ABOVE
Love for God

We cannot control people or the outcome of situations (Eccles. 3:1-11, 7:13-14, 9:1-2). We can only control our own thoughts, emotions, desires, words, and actions (Rom. 12:2-3, Prov. 16:32, Ps. 37:4, Eph. 4:29, 22-24). Therefore, we need to evaluate and take responsibility for how we are responding to people and the outcome of situations (Gal. 6:7-8, 5:16-25). We need to evaluate what is motivating us with people and the outcome of situations (Jas. 1:13-14, 3:13-16, 4:1-3). Are we motivated by love for God above our selfish desires? Or are we motivated by our selfish desires above love for God? (1 John 2:15-16; James 4:4, 3:16).

Scenarios

As you have learned the principle of what you cannot and can control, take time to work through a few scenarios of your life using this principle.

Part 1: What was the situation? Who, what, when, where, why?

Part 2: Identify what you could not control in the situation. The other person's specific thoughts, emotions, desires, words, or actions in the situation.

Part 3: Identify what you could control in the situation. Your specific thoughts, emotions, desires, words, or actions in the situation.

Part 4: Identify what motives determined your specific thoughts, emotions, desires, words, or actions in the situation. (My selfish desires or my love for God or for the person)

What Do You Want and How Are You Responding?

1. I Want _____ from _____:

a. _____

b. _____

c. _____

d. _____

e. _____

2. However, I end up getting _____ from _____:

a. _____

b. _____

c. _____

d. _____

e. _____

3. As a result I tend to react negatively by:

a. In my thoughts I think things such as / I feel things such as:

_____

b. In my conversation I say things such as:

_____

c. In my actions I tend to behave and live like:

_____

d. In my relational patterns toward _____, I:

_____

4. If I were to look at this from God's perspective, He would probably view my reaction as:

_____

5. Read James 3:13-4:10. Based upon this insight what are six key things you need to consider in your situation?

Illustration of Point I

God-Centered

Slave of God

Romans 6:22: But now having been freed from sin and enslaved to God, you derive your benefit, resulting in sanctification, and the outcome, eternal life.

Psalm 119:105: Your word is a lamp to my feet, and a light to my path.

We have two choices in life. We either choose to be God-centered or self-centered. The more we choose to be self-centered, the more we are held captive by our sin. The more we choose to be God-centered, we are freed from sin but walk in slavery to God, resulting in God's glory and our greatest good.

Self-Centered

Slave of Sin

Proverbs 5:22: His own iniquities will capture the wicked, and he will be held with the cords of his sin.

2 Timothy 3:1-4: But realize this, that in the last days difficult times will come. For men will be lovers of self, lovers of money, boastful, arrogant, revilers, disobedient to parents, ungrateful, unholy, unloving, irreconcilable, malicious gossips, without self-control, brutal, haters of good, treacherous, reckless, conceited, lovers of pleasure rather than lovers of God.

Point of Choice

The Point of Choice

Key Point: At the end of the day, a person only has two choices: to be self-centered or God-centered. This drives every other issue in life he or she encounters. The more we choose to be self-centered, the more we are held captive by our sin. The more we choose to be God-centered, we are freed from sin but walk in slavery to God, resulting in God's glory and our greatest good. The condition of our lives is determined by the choices we have made in life. Genuine biblical counseling helps individuals to understand this reality and to pursue the choice of being God-centered.

I. We Choose to Be God-Centered or Self-Centered (Gal. 5:16-25). *(See Illustration of Point I.)*

A. When we are God-centered, we choose to live our lives for God, resulting in doing things according to God's standards (Ps. 119:105).

B. When we are self-centered, we choose to live our lives for ourselves, resulting in doing things according to our own agenda (2 Tim. 3:1-4).

C. When we choose to live for ourselves instead of living for God, we will live in slavery to sin (Prov. 5:22).

D. When we choose to live for God instead of living for ourselves, we live in slavery to God (Rom. 6:22).

Illustration of Point II

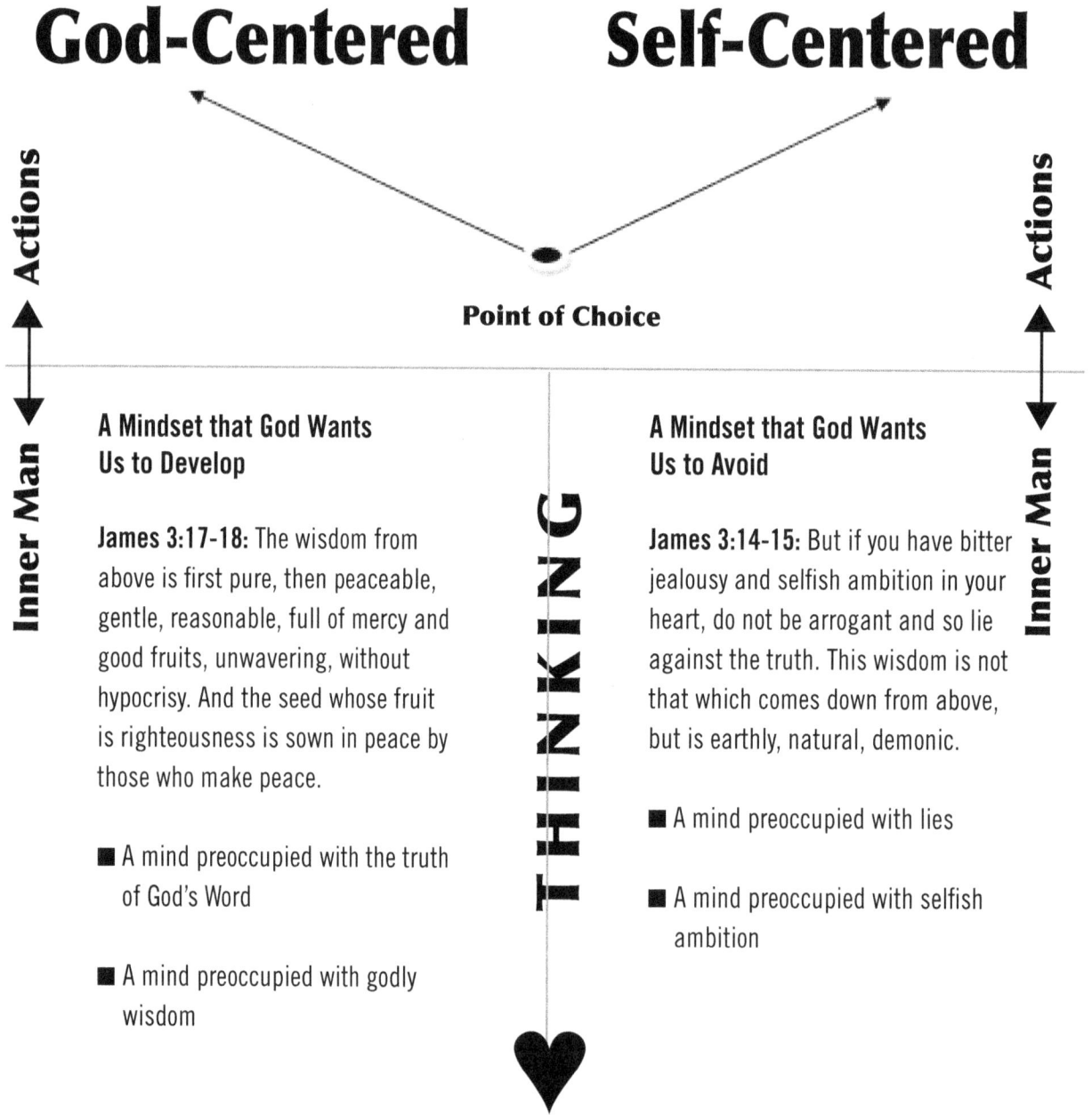

God-Centered

Self-Centered

Actions

Inner Man

Point of Choice

THINKING

Actions

Inner Man

A Mindset that God Wants Us to Develop

James 3:17-18: The wisdom from above is first pure, then peaceable, gentle, reasonable, full of mercy and good fruits, unwavering, without hypocrisy. And the seed whose fruit is righteousness is sown in peace by those who make peace.

- A mind preoccupied with the truth of God's Word

- A mind preoccupied with godly wisdom

A Mindset that God Wants Us to Avoid

James 3:14-15: But if you have bitter jealousy and selfish ambition in your heart, do not be arrogant and so lie against the truth. This wisdom is not that which comes down from above, but is earthly, natural, demonic.

- A mind preoccupied with lies

- A mind preoccupied with selfish ambition

II. Our choices are driven by our thoughts (Rom. 8:5). *(See illustration of Point II.)*

    A. When we are self-centered, our thoughts are dominated by lies and selfish ambition (Jas. 3:14-16).

    B. As a result of those lies and selfish ambition, our thoughts tend to be driven and reduced to what we have been denied, what we believe we deserve, what we want, what we think we should have, or what we think we need. We become friendly with the world and unfriendly with God (Jas. 4:1-10).

    C. When we are God-centered, our thoughts are dominated by truth and wisdom (Jas. 3:17-18).

    D. As a result of being dominated by truth and wisdom, our thoughts tend be driven by what God commands of us and how to live according to that. We focus on things such as what God promises to do for us and when to expect it. We tend also to focus on what God is doing for us and has done for us, as well as what we can be doing for others and how to do it appropriately (Jas. 3:13, 17-18).

Illustration of Point III

God   Self

Actions

Drawing near to God • Kindness
Self-control • Faith • Goodness
Patience • Love • Peace of God
Self-sacrificing • Humility •
Gentleness • Merciful • Wisdom
Joy • Confidence before God

Selfishness • Sense of Guilt
Sarcasm • Demanding • Anger •
Rage • Arrogance • Deceit • Fear
of Judgment • Liar • Cruelty •
Divisiveness • Abuse • Manipulative
• Jealousy • Hatred • Immorality •
Fleeing when no one is chasing

Galatians 5:16, 22-26   **Galatians 5:17-21**

Inner Man

Thoughts Motivated by the Holy Spirit

Desire to Know Jesus Christ

| Desire to become like Jesus Christ | Appreciating the blessings of God; Anticipating the return of Jesus Christ | Desire to be useful to Jesus Christ |

THINKING

Thoughts Motivated by the Flesh (Indwelling Sin)

Hedonism–Preoccupation with whatever brings me pleasure apart from God

| AUTONOMY Not having to answer to anyone | MATERIALISM Preoccupation with material things | ENTITLEMENT Believing I deserve whatever I want or pursue |

Romans 8:5b: "but those who are according to the Spirit, [set their minds on] the things of the Spirit."

Romans 8:5a: "Those who are according to the flesh set their minds on things of the flesh"

III. Our thoughts are motivated by the flesh (sin in our hearts) or by the Holy Spirit (Rom. 8:1-14). *(See illustration of Point III.)*

A. When our thoughts are motivated by the flesh (sin in our hearts), we are preoccupied with issues such as hedonism (whatever brings me pleasure apart from God), autonomy (independence from authority; not having to answer to anyone), materialism (love of material things), and entitlement (believing I deserve whatever I want or pursue) that dominate our thinking.

B. This leads to further disobedience to God. We will see attitudes and actions such as anger, hatred, immorality, jealousy, abuse, cruelty, lying, selfish ambition, arrogance, rage, sarcasm, or selfishness. This leads to a guilty conscience, a fear of God's judgment, and a desire to escape God's judgment, which result in our trying to flee from the inevitable consequences of disobedience to God (2 Tim. 3:1-9, Prov. 28:1).

C. When our thoughts are motivated by the Holy Spirit, we tend to be preoccupied with a desire to know Jesus Christ, to become like Jesus Christ, to be useful to Jesus Christ, the return of Jesus Christ, and the blessings in this life and the life to come from Jesus Christ our Lord.

D. This leads to further obedience to God. We will see attitudes and actions such as humility, patience, peace, joy, self-sacrifice, kindness, goodness, mercy, love, faith, gentleness, self-control, and wisdom. This leads to a peaceful conscience, a confidence in the presence of God, and a desire to draw near to God, which results in our drawing near to God (Gal. 5:22-25).

Illustration of Point IV and V

To Be

Appreciated Great

To Have Influence

Loved Accepted Served

To Never Hurt Again

In Charge Happy Approved of

Understood Satisfied Significant

Comfortable Safe Respected

To Have Our Way

Held in High Regard

Viewed as Competent

To Have Control

**Desires We Treasure and Worship Above
Loving God and Loving Others**

IV. When our thoughts are driven by the flesh (sin in our hearts) we will begin to worship our desires, turning them into the lusts of our lives (Jas. 4:1-3). *(See Illustration of Points IV and V)*

A. Our minds will be set on things below instead of things above, leading us to make self-interest a priority over God's will. We focus less and less on loving God and loving others; we focus more and more on using God and using others according to our self-interest (Phil. 3:17-19, Jas. 3:13-4:3).

B. Our desires will become preoccupations, resulting in our looking for avenues to satisfy these desires we have started to worship. We look to any person, place, product, or perspective we believe will satisfy these desires above loving God and loving others (Jas. 4:1-3).

C. We will build our lives around these desires we have started to worship above loving God and loving others (Phil. 3:17-19).

D. We will become servants of our flesh to satisfy these desires we have started to worship above loving God and loving others (Gal. 5:16-21).

V. As we make choices according to the desires we have begun to worship, we will find ourselves on a path of difficulty and hard times (Prov. 13:15). *(See Illustration of Points IV and V.)*

A. We will become a slave to that which we pursue above loving God and loving others (2 Peter 2:18-19).

B. We will develop sinful habits that are hard to repent of and replace as a result of pursuing those desires we worship above loving God and loving others (Prov. 5:21-22).

C. We will reap negative consequences of our sinful habits and pursuit of those desires we worship above loving God and loving others (Gal. 6:7-8).

D. We will have a negative effect on the lives of those around us as a result of pursuing those desires we worship above loving God and loving others (1 Cor. 5:1-6).

What Is the Situation?

What is happening? When? Where? With whom?

What do you want that you're not getting? What are you getting that you don't want?

Are you God-Centered or Self-Centered?

God-Centered

Self-Centered

8 What feelings are you displaying that reflect God-centeredness?

What words are you expressing that display God-centeredness?

What behaviors are you displaying that reveal God-centeredness?

What ways are you relating that display God-centeredness?

1 What feelings are you displaying that reflect self-centeredness?

What words are you expressing that display self-centeredness?

What behaviors are you displaying that reveal self-centeredness?

What ways are you relating that display self-centeredness?

7 What God-centered desires need to replace the self-centered desires?

THINKING

5 What God-centered thoughts need to replace the self-centered thoughts?

6 What God-centered motives need to replace the self-centered motives?

4 What are your self-centered desires?

2 What are your self-centered thoughts?

THINKING

3 What are your self-centered motives?

WALK IN THE SPIRIT

RECOGNIZE REPENT and REPLACE

Luke 9:23-25
1 John 1:9
Ephesians 4:17-24
Philippians 2:5
Colossians 3:5-7
Galatians 5:16, 22-23

VI. We must turn from a self-centered life to a God-centered life through the person, power, and precepts of Jesus Christ (Rom. 13:8-14). *(See Illustrations of Point VI.)*

A. We must identify the areas of our lives where we are dominated by lies, selfish ambition, hedonism, autonomy, materialism, entitlement, and lustful pursuits above loving God and loving others. We must identify where this is happening in our attitudes, intentions, desires, words, actions, relationship patterns, and service to God, and confess and repent of these things (Prov. 28:13-14).

B. We must decide to make God a priority in all that we think, say, and do (1 Cor. 10:31).

C. The areas of lives where we are dominated by lies, selfish ambition, hedonism, autonomy, materialism, entitlement, and lustful pursuits must be replaced with specific obedience to God in those areas (Eph. 4:17-32, Col. 3:1-25).

D. In other words, we must guard our hearts from self-centeredness by walking in genuine love for God and love for others in our attitudes, intentions, desires, words, actions, relationship patterns, and service.

Illustration of Point VI

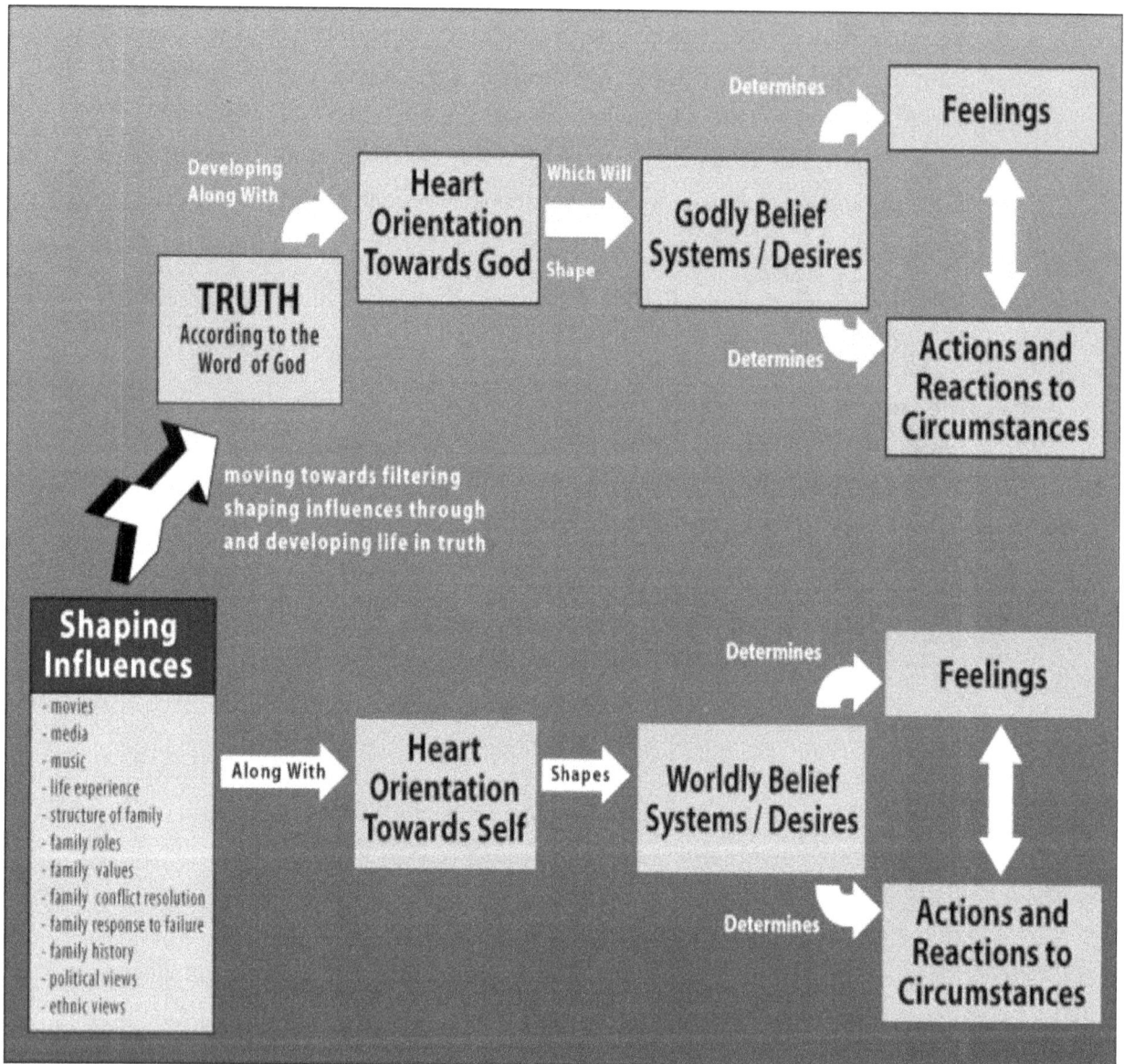

Developing Along With

Heart Orientation Towards God

Which Will Shape

TRUTH According to the Word of God

Godly Belief Systems / Desires

Determines

Feelings

Determines

Actions and Reactions to Circumstances

moving towards filtering shaping influences through and developing life in truth

Shaping Influences

- movies
- media
- music
- life experience
- structure of family
- family roles
- family values
- family conflict resolution
- family response to failure
- family history
- political views
- ethnic views

Along With

Heart Orientation Towards Self

Shapes

Worldly Belief Systems / Desires

Determines

Feelings

Determines

Actions and Reactions to Circumstances

Graphics by Adrian Baxter

Discussion Questions

1. When looking at the choices that you have made today, were you self-centered or God-centered in your choices? Write down your findings.

2. Identify your thought patterns that are rooted in lies and selfish ambition, then identify your thought patterns that are rooted in truth and godly wisdom. Explain how these thought patterns determined your choices above.

3. What desires have you allowed to become a form of worship, resulting in further complications in your life?

4. What loving thoughts, motives, desires, words, actions, relationship patterns, and service do you need to walk in to replace your sin?

Developing in Love for God and Love for Others

The First and Greatest Commandment
John 14:21-23

Definition of Love for God: To have a high regard for, a sincere value of, a committed devotion to, a genuine joy in, resulting in the act of the will in submitting to the will and directives of God

I. To love God is to *obey* His *commands* out of a pure heart, good conscience, and sincere faith; it is not a burden (1 Tim. 1:5, 1 John 5:3).

    A. To obey His commands means to faithfully/consistently (not perfectly) adhere to and ***follow*** the will and directions given by God as a way of life.

    B. To obey His commands is an act of the ***will*** that moves into action to do what is instructed by God on a faithful/consistent basis (not perfectly) as a way of life.

    C. To obey His commands does not arrive from a ***slavish fear*** of his directives but a willing submission to the instructions and directions of God as a way of life.

II. If we love God by *obeying* His *commands*, it will result in *experiencing* more of God's love toward us and His presence with us (Phil. 4:9, John 15:10-11, Ps. 16:11, Eph. 3:14-19).

A. As we walk in love for God the Father and God the Son through genuine obedience, we will come to experience ***deeper dimensions*** of God's love toward us.

B. As we walk in love for God the Father and God the Son through genuine obedience, we will come to experience a ***deeper reality*** of the presence of Jesus Christ, resulting in our experiencing more of the person, character, and goodness of Jesus Christ.

C. As we walk in love for God the Father and God the Son through genuine obedience, they will make themselves at home in our hearts, being the ***resident Masters*** that direct our attitudes and conduct accordingly as we experience the work of rooting and grounding us in love by God the Holy Spirit.

III. If we have a genuine love for God, it will not be demonstrated by merely *talking* about God and His Word. It will be revealed through our willing and consistent *obedience* to God through submission to His Word (Rom. 6:17-18; 1 John 2:3-6, 3:1-10; Luke 6:40, 43-49).

A. Genuine obedience is demonstrated by ***acceptance*** of the person and work of Jesus Christ to save us from the penalty of sin, power of sin, and soon the presence of sin, resulting in our becoming a slave to God instead of slave to sin.

B. Genuine obedience is demonstrated by ***application*** of God's command in all aspects of life. These aspects include:

1. ***Character***—to reflect the personality of God on the inside and outside.

"That in reference to your former manner of life, you lay aside the old self, which is being corrupted in accordance with the lusts of deceit, and that you be renewed in the spirit of your mind, and put on the new self, which in the likeness of God has been created in righteousness and holiness of truth" (Eph. 4:21-24).

2. **Conduct**—to carry yourself in a manner that represents the holiness of God and not self-righteousness or self-indulgence.

"As obedient children, do not be conformed to the former lusts which were yours in your ignorance, but like the Holy One who called you, be holy yourselves also in all your behavior, because it is written 'You shall be Holy for I Am Holy'" (1 Peter 1:14-16).

"Therefore if you have been raised up with Christ, keep seeking the things above, where Christ is seated at the right hand of God. Set your mind on things above, not on the things that are on the earth" (Col. 3:1-2).

3. **Conversation**—to speak words and to have dialogue that displays the character of God.

"Let no unwholesome word come out of your mouth, but if there is any good word for edification according to the need of the moment, say that, so that it will give grace to those who hear" (Eph. 4:29).

4. **Commitments**—to devote yourself to God.

"Therefore I urge you, brethren, by the mercies of God, to present your bodies a living and holy sacrifice, acceptable to God, which is your spiritual service of worship" (Rom. 12:1).

"Go, therefore, and make disciples of all the nations, baptizing them in the name of the Father and the Son and the Holy Spirit, teaching them to follow all that I commanded you; and lo, I am with you always, even to the end of the age" (Matt. 28:19-20).

5. **Commodities**—to enjoy and share generously the resources God has provided you without putting your hope in these resources.

"Instruct those who are rich in this present world not to be conceited or to fix their hope on the uncertainty of riches, but on God, who richly supplies us with all things to enjoy. Instruct them to do good, to be rich in good works, to be generous and ready to share" (1 Tim. 6:17-18).

6. **Communion**—to stay in consistent fellowship with other believers.

"And let us consider how to stimulate one another to love and good deeds, not forsaking our own assembling together, as is the habit of some, but encouraging one another; and all the more as you see the day drawing near" (Heb. 10:24-25).

The Second Great Commandment
A Fresh Dimension to an Old Commandment: John 13:34-35

I. The *Calling* to *Agape* [ah-GAH-peh] Love (John 13:34-35)

A. The word *new* in the text means a "fresh dimension."

B. The "fresh dimension" to the old command was that love is to be given in the sacrificial manner that Jesus gave to the believers.

C. The selfless service and sacrifice of His life as a ransom for others was altogether new, and consequently the model and standard for which their love for one another was to be measured.

D. In essence, we are called by the power of God to seek the highest good for others unconditionally, no strings attached.

E. We are called to respond to the condition and need of others above the attractiveness of and our personal interest in others.

F. We are called to have a genuine concern and benevolence toward others.

II. The *Considerations* of Agape Love

A. Agape love is not something we have to work up to give; it's something we work out through the power of the Holy Spirit within us (Gal. 5:22-23).

B. Agape love is not a continuum that flows automatically through us; it is developed through practice or derailed through disobedience to God (1 John 2:9-11).

C. Agape love is not given according to the character of the receiver but is given according to the character of the giver (1 John 3:11-24).

D. Agape love is an unlimited resource from the nature of God from which we can draw at any time; therefore we have no excuse not to love others with agape love (1 John 4:7).

E. It is hypocritical to expect agape love from others but not be willing to give agape love to others; we must be willing to give what we ask for (Luke 6:27-36).

F. The evidence of our Christianity is revealed by the agape love we demonstrate to others through the power of God (1 John 4:15-17).

III. The *Confusion* about Agape Love (1 Cor. 13:1-3)

A. Agape love is not merely using your spiritual gifts toward others.

B. Agape love is not merely giving of your resources to others.

C. Agape love is not merely sacrificing yourself for others.

D. All these things can be done for the wrong motives.

E. Ability, service, and sacrifice without agape love become a tool for self-promotion and self-advancement (Luke 18:9-14).

F. Ability, service, and sacrifice without agape love lead to self-deception about who you are and where you are with God (Luke 18:9-14).

IV. The *Clarity* of Agape Love

A. *Agape*—love that is based upon the power of God to seek the highest of good of others unconditionally, no strings attached.

B. Agape love is concerned not with how we feel but how we choose to think and act toward another.

C. Agape love responds not to the attractiveness of the other person but to the condition and need of the other person.

D. Agape love's motivation is not the selfish desire to enjoy the other person but the selfless desire to benefit him or her.

E. Essentially, agape love is concerned and benevolent toward others in attitude and action.

Key Point: There is no use trying to do church work without love. A doctor or a lawyer may do good work without love, but God's work cannot be done without love. Without love, our most extraordinary gifts and highest achievements are ultimately fruitless to the church and before God. Nothing has lasting spiritual value unless it springs from love.

V. The *Characteristics* of Agape Love (1 Cor. 13:4-8)

A. Agape love is patient. It suffers long and is able to put up with people, their issues, and the issues they bring into our lives for a long period of time and in the proper way without our responding in a hastily sinful response internally and externally.

B. Agape love is kind. It is genuine, sincere, and willing in attitude as well as genuine and sincere in the actions of ministering good and showing compassion toward others unconditionally for the glory of God and the blessing of others without looking for anything in return to self from others.

C. Agape love is not jealous. There is no demeanor of dissatisfaction, rivalry, or dislike toward others due to the fact or thought that they are or seem to be ahead of you, above you, superior to you, or have something you treasure at a level above you. This love is happy for others in their advancements ahead of you, achievements superior to you, accomplishments above you, or acquisitions of things you treasure but do not have or do not have at the level of that person.

D. Agape love does not brag. It does not promote itself but rather seeks to promote and praise God and others above self.

E. Agape love is not arrogant. It does not think of self as more important than others, better than others, or the creator and sustainer of all his/her own abilities, accomplishments, knowledge, blessings, liberties, benefits, or experiences. Love has a right view of self, according to his/her position before God and before others with a submissive and servant heart toward God and others, as empowered and commanded by God to do so.

F. Agape love does not act unbecomingly. It is not rude, rash, impolite, indecent, insensitive, inconsiderate, disrespectful, or dishonorable in words, behavior, or actions toward others but is considerate, courteous, respectable, right, decent, delicate, sensitive, and sympathetic in words, behavior, and actions toward others for the glory of God and the benefit of others.

G. Agape love does not seek its own. It does not live to please self but lives to please God, seeking the greatest good of others for God's glory and for other people's utmost welfare.

H. Agape love is not provoked. It is not irritated, not easily annoyed, not easily upset, or quick to have a fit in difficult situations with people or in difficult situations in life. Love is peaceful in disposition, calm, and gentle in difficult situations with people or in difficult situations in life.

I. Agape love does not take into account a wrong suffered. It does not keep a list in mind with the intent to get back at the person for the sinful, troublesome, painful, or disappointing activities a person has done against him or her. Love has a mindset of compassion in relation to the one who has wronged him or her intentionally, unintentionally, actually or imagined. Love is willing and ready to forgive according to God's design.

J. Agape love does not rejoice in unrighteousness but rejoices with the truth. It does not take joy in, take pleasure in, or find satisfaction in evil or unrighteousness of any kind but it takes joy in, takes pleasure in, and finds satisfaction in right living practiced by others and the triumphs of others as they practice right living.

K. Agape love bears all things. It does not give way to the temptation to respond in sin to the pressure put on him or her by others via their sinful attitudes, strange or unusual ways, or personal preferences, but rather seeks to do what is right by them or to them according to the need of the moment consistently.

L. Agape love believes all things. It seeks to understand people in the best possible light without ignoring or disregarding their proven character flaws and sin issues. Love stays away from developing a suspicious, cynical, doubtful, skeptical, fault-finding, judgmental, or hypercritical pattern of thinking about others as result of their proven character flaws and sin issues.

M. Agape love hopes all things. No matter what the situation, love considers the bright side of things for others by looking to the grace of God in relation to them.

N. Agape love endures all things. Love continues to do what is right with and for people and in all circumstances, even when facing difficulty or hardships.

Evaluate the roles you have in life and identify ways you can be open and loving within that role to others (1 Cor. 13:4-8).

Various Roles I have in life	Loving Thoughts I should have toward others in this role	Loving Words I should say to others in this role	Loving Service I should do toward others in this role	Any other things I can think of
Husband/Father				
Wife/Mother				
Child				
Brother				
Sister				
Aunt/Uncle				
Niece				
Nephew				

Various Roles I have in Life	Loving Thoughts I should have toward others in this role	Loving Words I should say to others in this role	Loving Service I should do toward others in this role	Any other things I can think of
Grandfather				
Grandmother				
Cousin				
Mother-in-law				
Father-in-law				
Son-in-law				
Daughter-in-law				
Friend				

Various Roles I have in Life	Loving Thoughts I should have toward others in this role	Loving Words I should say to others in this role	Loving Service I should do toward others in this role	Any other things I can think of
Co-worker				
Employer				
Employee				
Enemy				
Neighbor				
Authority figure				
Subordinate				

Various Resources

An author or speaker seldom arrives at completely original thoughts while also being able to communicate them clearly. I am indebted to many inspiring teachers and authors who have informed my own understanding and development of this workbook's topics.

Listed below are the persons and resources, in order of their appearance in the workbook, whose ideas I greatly appreciate and acknowledge as the springboards for some of my thoughts and teaching. (Most resources also appear in the Bibliography, but a few could not be included there, due to lack of complete source information.)

Section 1 XI F: Tripp, *Instruments in the Redeemer's Hands*

    XII A-E: Randy Patten

    XIV A-D: Jay Adams

    XVI A, D: David Powlison

Section 3 XIV: Graphics and summary, Keith and Jujuan Bowen

Section 4: Consent to Counsel Form, Wayne Mack Ministries

Section 5 VII: Tripp, *Instruments in the Redeemer's Hands*

Section 6: Salvation Concepts to Teach

    Initial graphic: Matt Silva

Section 10: Thomson, *The Heart of Man and the Mental Disorders*

      II B, IV D: Berger, *Rethinking Depression*

Section 11 VII: Key Point: Berger, *Rethinking Depression*

Section 13, Illustrations for Points I and II: Mark Dutton

      First Illustration for Point VI: John Street

Section 14, The Second Great Commandment, I: Jamieson, Fausset, and Brown

      IV E: Boyer, *For a World Like Ours*

      IV F: Strauch, *A Christian Leader's Guide to Leading with Love*, pp. 8, 16

      V I: Thomson, *The Heart of Man and the Mental Disorders*

      V J: Mack, *Maximum Impact*

Bibliography

Adams, Jay E. *Christian Counselor's Manual: The Practice of Nouthetic Counseling.* Grand Rapids: Zondervan, 1986.

———. *Encouragement Isn't Enough.* Stanley, NC: Timeless Texts, 2007.

———. *How to Help People Change.* Grand Rapids: Zondervan, 1986.

Berger, Daniel II. *Rethinking Depression: Not a Sickness Not a Sin.* Taylors, SC: Alethia International Publications, 2019.

Boyer. *For a World Like Ours: Studies in I Corinthians.* Grand Rapids: Baker Book House, 1971.

Jamieson, Robert, A.R. Fausset, David Brown. *A Commentary, Critical and Explanatory, on the Old and New Testaments.* Oak Harbor, WA: Logos Research Systems, Inc., 1997.

Mack, Wayne A. *Maximum Impact: Living and Loving for God's Glory* (Phillipsburg, N.J.: P&R Pub., 2010.

Strauch, Alexander. *A Christian Leader's Guide to Leading with Love.* Littleton, CO: Lewis & Roth Publishers, 2002.

Thomson, Rich. *The Heart of Man and the Mental Disorders*, Houston: Biblical Counseling Ministries, Inc., 2004.

———.MSBC 4343 Biblical Counseling Course at the College of Biblical Studies, Houston, Texas).

Tripp, Paul David. *Instruments in the Redeemer's Hands: People in Need of Change Helping People in Need of Change.* Phillipsburg, NJ: P&R Publ., 2002.

www.ingramcontent.com/pod-product-compliance
Lightning Source LLC
Chambersburg PA
CBHW080337270326
41927CB00014B/3254